A Treasury of Ḥadīth

THE TREASURY SERIES IN
ISLAMIC THOUGHT AND CIVILIZATION

I. *A Treasury of Ḥadīth*, Ibn Daqīq al-ʿĪd

II. *A Treasury of Ghazālī*, Mustafa Abu Sway

III. *A Treasury of Islamic Legal Maxims*, Dr. Shahrul Hussain

IV. *A Treasury of Ibn Taymiyyah*, Mustapha Sheikh

V. *A Treasury of Al-Rūmī*, Dr. Isa Waley (Forthcoming)

VI. *A Treasury of Iqbāl*, Abdur Rashid Siddiqui (Forthcoming)

Ibn Daqīq al-ʿĪd

A Treasury of Ḥadīth

A Commentary on Nawawī's Forty Prophetic Traditions

Translated by
Mokrane Guezzou

KUBE PUBLISHING

A Treasury of Ḥadīth
A Commentary on
Nawawī's Forty Prophetic Traditions

First published in England by
Kube Publishing Ltd
Markfield Conference Centre
Ratby Lane, Markfield
Leicestershire LE67 9SY
United Kingdom

TEL +44 (0)1530 249230
FAX +44 (0)1530 249656
WEBSITE www.kubepublishing.com
EMAIL info@kubepublishing.com

5th impression,2024

CIP data for this book is available from the British Library.

ISBN 978-1-84774-067-0 casebound
ISBN 978-1-84774-069-4 ebook

Cover design Inspiral Design
Book design & typesetting Imtiaze Ahmed
Arabic typesetting Naiem Qaddoura
Printed in Turkey by Elma Basim

Contents

Imām Nawawī's Introduction

In the Name of Allah, Most Merciful and Compassionate

PRAISE BE TO God, Lord of the Worlds, the Sustainer of the heavens and earths, the Disposer of all created beings, the Sender of Messengers, may God's blessing and peace be upon them, to those who are legally responsible, so as to guide them and elucidate [to them] the ordinances of the religion with conclusive proofs and clear evidences. I praise Him for all His blessings, and ask Him for more of His favour and generosity.

I also bear witness that there is no deity but God, the One, the All-Compelling, the Generous and the Oft-Forgiving. And I bear witness that Muhammad is His servant and messenger, beloved and intimate friend, the best of all created beings, who was honoured with the noble Qur'ān – the continuous miracle throughout the years – and with clear ways for those seeking guidance; and who was further singled out to have the most comprehensive speech and tolerance of religion. And may God's blessings and peace be upon him and upon all the prophets, their households and upon all the righteous among people.

To proceed: we have narrated from ʿAlī ibn Abī Ṭālib, ʿAbd Allāh ibn Masʿūd, Muʿādh ibn Jabal, Abū'l-Dardā', Ibn ʿUmar, Ibn ʿAbbās, Anas ibn Mālik, Abū Hurayrah and

Abū Saʿīd al-Khudrī, may God be pleased with them, from many chains of transmission and in variegated versions that God's Messenger, may God's blessings and peace be upon him, said: 'Whosoever preserves for my Community forty *aḥādīth* relating to matters of its religion, God will resurrect him on Judgement Day with the scholars of Sacred Law and the scholars of sacred knowledge', and, in another version, 'God will resurrect him as a scholar of Sacred Law and sacred knowledge.' The version of Abū'l-Dardā' has 'and I shall be a witness and intercessor for him on Judgement Day'; and, in the version of Ibn Masʿūd, 'he shall be told: enter from any of the gates of Paradise you wish to enter'; and, in the version of Ibn ʿUmar, 'he shall be recorded amongst the group of scholars of sacred know- ledge and assembled amongst the martyrs'. *Ḥadīth* masters are in agreement that this *ḥadīth* is weak even though its chains of transmission are diverse.

Scholars, may God be pleased with them, have authored countless books in this field. The first I know of who has written in this field is ʿAbd Allāh ibn al-Mubārak, then Muḥammad ibn Aslam al-Ṭūsī, the pious scholar, then al-Ḥasan ibn Sufyān al-Nasawī, Abū Bakr al-Ājūrī, Abu Bakr Muḥammad ibn Ibrāhīm al-Aṣfahānī, al-Dāraquṭnī, al-Ḥākim, Abū Nuʿaym [al-Aṣfahānī], Abū ʿAbd al-Raḥmān al-Sulamī, Abu Saʿīd al-Mālīnī, Abū ʿUthman al-Ṣābūnī, ʿAbd Allāh ibn Muḥammad al-Anṣārī, Abū Bakr al-Bayhaqī, and countless other people from the first and later generations of Muslims. Hence, I have sought God's guidance to gather forty prophetic sayings in emulation of these eminent masters and preservers of Islam.

The scholars of sacred knowledge are in agreement about the permissibility of using weak prophetic traditions as evidence for performing works of virtue. Nonetheless, my reliance is not on this above-mentioned tradition. I am rather relying on his saying, may God's blessings and peace be upon him, in rigorously-authenticated *aḥādīth*: 'let those present among you inform those who are absent', and on his saying, may God's blessings and peace be upon him, 'God bestows beauty and light on the person who hears my speech, remembers it and then passes it on as he has heard it.'

Furthermore, there are among the scholars of sacred knowledge those who have gathered forty *aḥādīth* relating to tenets of faith, while others chose particular questions of Sacred Law, or jihad, or non-attachment, or good conduct, or the sermons of the Prophet, may God's blessings and peace be upon him – all of which are noble aims, may God be pleased with those who sought to compile them.

I have decided to compile forty *aḥādīth* that are more important than all these aims and which further comprise all of them. Each *ḥadīth* is a great rule of the religion, described by scholars of sacred knowledge as an axis of Islam, or that it is half of Islam or its third, or something similar. In these forty *aḥādīth*, I confine myself to those rigorously authenticated, most of which are in the rigorously-authenticated collections of Bukhārī and Muslim. I shall mention them without their chains of transmission so as to facilitate their memorization and widen their benefit, God willing, and then I shall follow them by a chapter in which I explain difficult words.

Anyone desiring the Afterlife ought to know these *aḥādīth* in view of what they contain of important matters and of reminder of all acts of obedience; this is obvious to anyone who has bothered to think. My reliance is on God, I seek refuge in Him and to Him I consign my affairs. Praise and blessing are His, and through Him is success and protection from sin.

Ibn Daqīq al-ʿĪd's Commentary on Nawawī's Introduction

I*n the Name of Allah, Most Merciful and Compassionate*), that is to say: in the name of He Who is truly worshipped, the Necessary Existent, the Creator who creates out of magnanimity and generosity, I write in 'the Name of Allah, the Most Merciful, the Compassionate'. The Most Merciful (*al-Raḥmān*) means He Whose general mercy extends to all creation, while the Compassionate (*al-Raḥīm*) means He Whose special mercy is only for the faithful. The origin of compassion is the inclination of the heart and also tenderness, but in relation to Allah, may He be glorified and exalted, it means willing goodness for those who deserve it, or refraining from punishing those who have committed a punishable act.

The author, may Allah have mercy on him, began his book with mentioning the name of God and praising him in emulation of the Glorious Qur'ān and acting upon the rigorously-authenticated, beneficial prophetic tradition, 'Any matter of importance not begun by "in the Name of Allah, the Most Merciful, the Compassionate" or by "praise be to Allah", or by praising Allah, or by mentioning Allah, is cut off, or inconclusive or incomplete', according to different versions, which all convey the meaning that any matter in which the mention of the Name of Allah (*tasmiyyah*) is left out is of little blessing (*barakah*) or is deprived of any increase. The version of the saying that has 'by mentioning Allah' is more comprehensive.

Most scholars agree that the name of majesty (*Allah*) is God's greatest name. It is therefore a proper name of the Most Holy Divine Essence who deserves all kinds of praise. It is for this reason that the author said (*praise be to Allah*), i.e., graceful eulogy and commendation are due to Allah. (*Lord*), i.e., Sovereign, Creator, Disposer and Master. (*The worlds*), what is predominantly meant here are the intelligible worlds, for it is a term that covers anything other than Allah. However this term (*worlds*) is not applied to individuals such that one cannot say, 'Zayd is a world,' save figuratively. (*The Sustainer of the heavens*), means the One in charge of running and preserving them. Allah Most High says, *God holds the heavens and the earth, lest they remove* [*Fāṭir* 35: 39]. (*And the earths*), the plural of earth. (*The Disposer of Created Beings*), i.e., the Disposer of the affairs of created beings, since He knows the ultimate ends of their matters. (*He sent to those who are legally responsible*), i.e., he was sent to all of them. (*May God's blessings and peace be upon him*) means: O Allah! Send blessings and salutations on him. In some copies this is mentioned in the singular, i.e., (*May God's blessing and peace be upon him*). This sending of salutation (*taṣliyyah*) is from the root (*ṣilah*), i.e., connection, and so when it proceeds from the servant it is a supplication of seeking connection to and proximity with Allah. Our salutation on the Messenger is a request for a suitable connection and a tremendous Divine gift to him from God for the blessing that He has bestowed upon us because of him, may Allah's blessings and peace be upon him. It is also said that coming from God, the salutation on the Prophet, God's blessings and peace be upon him, means mercy enjoined with exaltation. (*His salutation*), i.e., His greeting which behoves their exalted honour.

His saying (*for their guidance*) means: for directing people to the path of guidance, which also follows from his saying (*the Sender*). (*Divine Sacred Laws*), the Arabic word is from *sharaʿa*, which means 'to show'; it means both way of life (*Dīn*) and religion (*millah*). One singles out either meaning only when taking into consideration which specific aspect one wants to stress. The legal rulings insofar as we are introduced and rewarded for them are (*Dīn*); and insofar as the Angel relates them to the Messenger and the Messenger relates them to us, they are *millah*; and insofar as they are laid bare and explained to us, they are *sharʿ* and *sharīʿah*.

The *Dīn* is a Divine stipulation that leads those possessed of minds, through their good choice, to that which is good for them in itself. (*With conclusive proofs*) refers to (*elucidate*) and it means the kind of proofs that puts an end to the argumentation of the opponent, because it comes from Allah. (*Clear evidences*), i.e., demonstrations that are clear. Their conjunction with (*conclusive proofs*) follows the usage of annexing that which is of particular applicability to that which is of general applicability. This is because a demonstration is composed of two judgements, which, when these are sound, inherently necessitate a third one. An example of this is: The world is ever-changing, and anything that changes is contingent, so it follows that the world is contingent. As for proof, it is that whose know- ledge necessitates the knowledge of something else, whether it is compound like the previous example or simple such as saying: these created beings are proof for the existence of Allah, Most High.

(*I praise Him*), i.e., I laud Him once more for all His blessings. And so the author mentioned praise first in conjunction with the Most Holy Divine Essence which is characterized by all His attributes, and again in conjunction with all His successive blessings. He used a nominal sentence with the first, which denotes continuity and uninterruptedness, and a verbal sentence with the second, which denotes renewal and successiveness, to give each context that which it deserves.

(*More*), i.e., more blessings such that the article of definition (*al-*) in (*al-mazīd*) is a substitute for an object of the sentence. (*Of His favour*), a favour is what is given out of choice, not out of necessity, i.e., something that takes place by nature without one having a choice in the matter, as the sages would say, not out of necessity as claimed by the Muʿtazilites. As for generosity, it is giving abundantly without any reason.

(*And I bear witness*), i.e., I certify and submit that (*there is no god*), i.e., there is none worshipped truly with all kinds of acts of worship (*except Allah*). (*The Oft-Forgiving*), *al-Ghaffār* (Oft-Forgiving) is derived from *ghafr* which means concealing faults. (*And that Muhammad*), Muhammad is derived from *al-ḥamd* (praise) due to his abundant praiseworthy traits. (*Is His servant*), the author started first with this description (i.e., servanthood) because it is the most honourable of stations. It is for this reason that Allah has referred to the Prophet, God's blessings and peace be upon him, with this agnomen in the most splendid utterance when He said, *Glory be to Him, who carried His servant by night from the Holy Mosque to the Further Mosque* [*al-Isrā'* 17: 1] and He also said, *When the servant of God stood calling on Him* [*Nūḥ* 71: 17]. For the genuine servant vis-à-vis his Lord is he whose heart is free from any desire for humiliation or submission to other than Him. (*Beloved*), i.e., the lover and the one who is loved; (*and intimate friend*), *khalīl* is from *khulla*, which means pure love that permeates the heart. (*And with clear ways for those seeking guidance*), i.e., with that which has been prescribed by the Prophet, may Allah bless him and give him peace, being the Lawgiver of legal prescriptions, whether obligatory or supererogatory, for those who seek correct conduct which is the opposite of misguidance. (*The most comprehensive speech*), in the sense that he condenses many meanings in few words; (*and tolerance of religion*), i.e., its easiness. Allah Most High says, *and has laid on you no impediment in your religion* [*al-Ḥajj* 22: 75]. This is in contrast to previous nations whereby the repentance of a person was not accepted until he killed himself, as mentioned by Allah Most High about the followers of Moses, *now turn to your Creator and slay one another* [*al-Baqarah* 2: 50].

(*May God's blessings and peace be upon him...*), the author mentions the formula of blessings and peace here on the Prophet, may Allah bless him and give him peace, in compliance with that which is in the Noble Qur'ān, (*and upon all...*), i.e., the remaining prophets.

It is related in the *Musnad* of Imām Aḥmad that the number of prophets sent by God is 124,000, among whom 315 are Messengers. All these prophets and messengers were non-Arabs and had non-Arab names, except for Muhammad, Hūd, Ṣāliḥ, and Shuʿayb. As for Ishmael, he is an Arab but his name is not. It is not obligatory to believe in all of them in details except for the twenty-five prophets and Messengers among them who are mentioned in *Sūrah al-Anʿām* in His saying Most High, *That is Our argument, which We bestowed upon Abraham as against his people. We raise up in degrees whom We will; surely thy Lord is All-Wise, All-Knowing. And We gave to him Isaac and Jacob – each one We guided, And Noah We guided before;*

and of his seed David and Solomon, Job and Joseph, Moses and Aaron – even so We recompense the good-doers – Zachariah and John, Jesus and Elias; each was of the righteous; Ishmael and Elisha, Jonah and Lot – each one We preferred above all beings; and of their fathers, and of their seed, and of their brethren; and We elected them, and We guided them to a straight path [*al-Anʿām* 6: 80–85]. Their precedence follows this order: Muhammad, Ibrāhīm, Mūsā, ʿĪsā, Nūḥ. (*And their households*), i.e., the household of each one of the prophets and messengers, i.e., their relatives who believed in them. But what is meant here is every single believer for it befits more the position of making supplications. (*And upon all the righteous people*), i.e., those who uphold the rights of God and the rights of His servants, which means that the prophetic Companions and others are included in this description.

(*We have narrated*) in the active form, i.e., we have transmitted from others. The sentence (*that God's Messenger, may God's blessings and peace be upon him...*) is its object (*mafʿūl*). (*Abū Hurayrah*), Hurayrah is the diminutive of *hirrah* (cat), the Prophet, may God's blessings and peace be upon him, gave him this nickname when he saw him holding a kitten in his sleeve. (*From many chains of transmission*) relates to 'we have narrated'. (*In variegated versions*), i.e., in different wordings. (*Whoever preserves*), i.e., transmits even if he does not memorize the exact words and does not understand their meaning. For it is through transmission that Muslims benefit, in contrast to that which is preserved but not transmitted to them. Thus was it related from the author. (*For my community*), i.e., for its sake and out of pity for it. What is meant here is the community of response, i.e., those who have accepted the message of Islam (*ummat al-ijābah*) not that of invitation, i.e. those invited to Islam but whom have not embraced it (*ummat al-daʿwah*), i.e., the whole world. (*Relating to matters of its religion*), i.e., relating to the principles or auxiliary matters of its religion. (*A witness*), i.e., a witness to his perfection. (*Martyrs*) those killed in the battlefield, or those whom God and the angels bear witness that they will enter Paradise.

What one learns from these different versions is that those who preserve forty prophetic sayings have different ranks. There are those who will be mustered with the scholars, and those who will be resurrected as scholars of Sacred Law even if they were not so in this world, while others are resurrected in different ranks.

The wisdom behind specifying the number forty in this prophetic saying is that it is the first number that has a rounded quarter of a tenth. Just as the prophetic saying relating to *zakāh* indicates that a quarter of the tenth cleanses the rest of one's property, so is acting upon a quarter of a tenth of forty prophetic sayings entails that the remainder are not left without being acted upon. Bishr al-Ḥāfī, may God be pleased with him, used to say: 'O folk of *Ḥadīth*! Out of every forty prophetic sayings, act on [at least] one of them.'

(Ḥadīth *masters are in agreement*), i.e., most of them (*that this* ḥadīth *is weak*), a weak prophetic saying is one in which some of the narrators are rejected due to their unreliability or because of narrating from someone they did not personally meet, or due to being known for their weak memory or being accused of having an unorthodox belief, or because they narrate from someone whose state they did not know, or due to some other reasons detailed in the books on the terminology of *Ḥadīth* (*muṣṭalaḥ al-ḥadīth*).

(*Even though its chains of transmission are diverse*), the chains are the narrators relating from other narrators up to the prophetic Companions, even if they happen to be among the less prominent among the prophetic Companions. The narrators are links in the chains of transmission that lead to the text of the prophetic saying. There is hardly any chain of transmission leading to a prophetic saying that is free from an unknown narrator, or from someone who is well known for his weakness. Describing a prophetic saying as being weak, authenticated or rigorously authenticated relates to its chains of transmission, i.e., the transmitters who narrated it. The prophetic saying whose chain of transmission is contiguous and its narrators reliable is an authenticated prophetic saying. Anything other than this is a weak prophetic saying. The weak prophetic sayings are divided into numerous categories.

(*In this field*), i.e., the field of gathering forty prophetic sayings. (*I have sought God's guidance*), i.e., I have requested Allah to guide me to what is better in relation to gathering or not gathering forty prophetic sayings. This is because he might have been occupied with acts of worship that are more important than gathering forty prophetic sayings. Just as the prayer for seeking guidance (*istikhārah*) is used for permissible matters (*mubāḥ*), it is also used for recommended (*mandūb*) matters to see which one takes precedence. The way of performing it is to pray two units of prayer and then supplicate with the well-known supplication which the Prophet, may God's blessings and peace be upon him, taught his Companions. This prayer of seeking guidance does not depend on what one subsequently sees in one's dream, rather it has to do with the inclination that one finds in one's heart after performing this prayer. The Prophet, may God's blessings and peace be upon him, said in the saying narrated by al-Ṭabarānī in *al-Awsaṭ* from Anas: 'He who seeks guidance will never go wrong, and he who consults others will never have any regrets, and he who saves up will never be impoverished.'

(*Works of virtue*), i.e., because if it is authentic in itself, then it is given its due right by acting upon it. Otherwise acting upon it will not culminate in any harm of declaring what is unlawful to be lawful or what is lawful to be unlawful. However, the condition for acting on a weak prophetic saying is that its weakness should not so severe such that none of its chains of transmission is free from a narrator who is a liar or someone accused of lying, and that it should also fit into a universal principle. An example of this is if there is a weak prophetic saying enjoining the performance of two units of prayer after noon (*zawāl*), then one acts on it because it fits into a universal principle which is the saying of the Prophet, may God's blessings and peace be upon him: 'The prayer is the best stipulated matter by God. Whoever is able to perform it abundantly, let him do so.'[1]

(*Nonetheless*), i.e., despite what was mentioned about the permissibility of acting upon weak prophetic sayings. (*Let the present*), i.e., the one who is hearing what I am saying. The address here is to the prophetic Companions, and then to those who come after them, and so on and so forth. It is therefore a collective obligation (*farḍ kifāyah*) on the people of knowledge to convey it. Anyone who has learnt a question is counted among the people of knowledge of this particular question, and it is obligatory on him to teach it to others. He becomes sinful if he fails to convey it in case no one else does so. (*And then passes it on*), i.e., literally or just its meaning, for it is permissible to narrate the meaning of a prophetic saying rather than narrating it word-for-word if such a narration complies with the condi- tion laid out by the scholars of *Ḥadīth*.

(*Tenets of faith*), what is meant here are questions relating to the Divine Essence and the function of prophecy, the Mustering and Resurrection. (*Particular questions of Sacred*

Knowledge), i.e., legal questions. (*Or jihad*), i.e., on the virtue of fighting the unbelievers. (*Or non-attachment*), i.e., on the virtue of abstaining from that which one does not have need of the stuff of this world. (*Or good conduct*), i.e., praiseworthy character traits, which include virtuous acts of behaviour that lead to the Most Generous Creator. (*The sermons of the Prophet, may God's blessings and peace be upon him*) which he delivered on occasions such as the Friday or ʿĪd prayers or upon the advent of serious events. The Arabs used to gather and listen to sermons whenever they faced hardship, so as to unite and help each other to overcome it.

(*Forty* aḥādīth), this is not refuted by the fact that Nawawī added two more prophetic sayings [as the collection contains forty-two sayings], and whoever adds more, God will add more to his good deeds. (*Rule of the religion*), i.e., one of the foundations of the religion. (*Axis of Islam*), i.e., most of its prescriptions revolve around it, such as the prophetic saying: 'The lawful is clear and the unlawful is clear.'[2] (*Half of Islam or its third*) such as the prophetic saying: 'Actions are but according to intention.'[3] Abū Dāwūd said: 'This saying amounts to half of Islam, for the religion consists of what is manifest, i.e., works, and that which is non-manifest, i.e., the intention.' As for Imām Shāfiʿī, it is reported that he said: 'This saying amounts to a third of it [Islam], for that which the servant acquires is either by his heart, his tongue or his limbs, and the intention is one of these three.' (*Or something similar*), i.e., a quarter of Islam, such as the prophetic saying: 'None of you shall truly believe until he loves for his brother what he loves for himself',[4] for it is said it amounts to a quarter of the religion.

(*Rigorously authenticated*), i.e., not weak, which means that authenticated *aḥādīth* (*ḥasan*) are also included. (*So as to facilitate their memorization*), i.e., the texts of the prophetic sayings since there is no benefit in mentioning the chains of transmission to many people once they know they are rigorously authenticated. (*Important matters*), which are the exposition of religious beliefs and the foundations of Divine prescriptions.

I

Works Are Only According to Intentions

عَنْ أَمِيرِ الْمُؤْمِنِينَ أَبِي حَفْصٍ عُمَرَ بْنِ الْخَطَّابِ رَضِيَ اللَّهُ عَنْهُ قَالَ: سَمِعْتُ رَسُولَ اللَّهِ صَلَّى اللَّهُ عَلَيْهِ وَسَلَّمَ يَقُولُ: إِنَّمَا الْأَعْمَالُ بِالنِّيَّاتِ، وَإِنَّمَا لِكُلِّ امْرِئٍ مَا نَوَى، فَمَنْ كَانَتْ هِجْرَتُهُ إِلَى اللَّهِ وَرَسُولِهِ فَهِجْرَتُهُ إِلَى اللَّهِ وَرَسُولِهِ، وَمَنْ كَانَتْ هِجْرَتُهُ لِدُنْيَا يُصِيبُهَا أَوْ امْرَأَةٍ يَنْكِحُهَا فَهِجْرَتُهُ إِلَى مَا هَاجَرَ إِلَيْهِ.

رَوَاهُ إِمَامَا الْمُحَدِّثِينَ أَبُو عَبْدِ اللهِ مُحَمَّدُ بْنُ إِسْمَاعِيل بن إِبْرَاهِيم بن الْمُغِيرَة بن بَرْدِزبَه الْبُخَارِيُّ الْجُعْفِيُّ [رقم:١]، وَأَبُو الْحُسَيْنِ مُسْلِمُ بْنُ الْحَجَّاج بن مُسْلِمِ الْقُشَيْرِيُّ النَّيْسَابُورِيُّ [رقم:١٩٠٧] رَضِيَ اللهُ عَنْهُمَا فِي صَحِيحَيْهِمَا اللَّذَيْنِ هُمَا أَصَحُّ الْكُتُبِ الْمُصَنَّفَةِ.

It is reported that the leader of the believers Abū Ḥafṣ ʿUmar ibn al-Khaṭṭāb – may God be pleased with him – said: I heard God's Messenger – may God's blessings and peace be upon him – saying, 'Verily works are only according to intentions, and each person

[gets] what he intends. Whosoever has migrated to God and His Messenger, his migration is to God and His Messenger; and whosoever has migrated to obtain a worldly means or to marry a woman, his migration is for the sake of what he has migrated for.'

This *ḥadīth* was narrated by the two masters of all *Ḥadīth* experts, Abū ʿAbd Allāh Muhammad ibn Ismāʿīl ibn Ibrāhīm ibn al-Mughīrah ibn Bardizbah al-Bukhārī al-Juʿfī and Abū'l-Ḥusayn Muslim ibn al-Ḥajjāj ibn Muslim al-Qushayrī al-Naysābūrī in their respective collections of rigorously-authenticated prophetic sayings, which are the most reliable books written in the field.

This is a rigorously-authenticated prophetic saying whose authentication, tremendous and exalted standing and abundant benefits are all agreed upon. Imām Abū ʿAbd Allāh al-Bukhārī narrated it in more than one place in his book. Abū'l-Ḥusayn Muslim ibn al-Ḥajjāj also narrated it at the end of the Book of Jihad. It is one of the prophetic sayings upon which Islam revolves. Both Imām Aḥmad and Imām Shāfiʿī stated that, 'In the prophetic saying: "Works are according to intentions..." is included a third of all [sacred] knowledge'; this was reported by Bayhaqī and others. The reason for this lies in the fact that what the servant acquires [of works] is limited to his heart, tongue or limbs, and the intention belongs to one of these three categories. It is also related from Imām Shāfiʿī that he said, 'Included in this prophetic saying are seventy subcategories of *fiqh*.' A group of scholars also said, 'This prophetic saying amounts to a third of Islam.'

The scholars have recommended that authored works start with this prophetic saying. Among the first to begin their works with this saying is Imām Abū ʿAbd Allāh al-Bukhārī. ʿAbd al-Raḥmān ibn Mahdī stated, 'It is incumbent upon everyone who authors a book to start it with this prophetic saying to alert the student of knowledge to correct his intention.'

This prophetic saying is well known (*mashhūr*) for its end, but peculiar (*gharīb*) for its beginning, for none related it from the Prophet, may God's blessings and peace be upon him, except ʿUmar ibn al-Khaṭṭāb, may Allah be well pleased with him, and none related it from ʿUmar except ʿAlqamah ibn Abī Waqqāṣ, and none related it from ʿAlqamah except Muhammad ibn Ibrāhīm al-Taymī, and none related it from Muhammad ibn Ibrāhīm except Yaḥyā ibn Saʿīd al-Anṣārī, after which it became well known as more than 200 people, most of whom were masters of *Ḥadīth*, related it from the latter.

The word (*innamā*) [only/naught/but] is used for delineation: it affirms what is mentioned and excludes everything else. Sometimes it denotes absolute delineation and sometimes restricted delineation which is understood from other indications (*qarā'in*) such as the words of God Most High, *You are only a warner* [*Raʿd* 13: 7]. The apparent meaning of this verse is that the Prophet, may God's blessings and peace be upon him, is delineated by his mission of warning. However, the Messenger, may God's blessings and peace be upon him, cannot be delineated by just this, for he has many other beautiful characteristics, such as bringing glad tidings (*bishārah*) and others. Likewise the words of God Most High, *The present life is naught but a sport and a diversion* [*Muhammad* 47: 36] seems, and Allah knows best, to be a demarcation if one takes into consideration those who prefer it to the next world. As for what it is in and of itself, it could well be a means to acts of goodness; the description used in the Qur'ānic verse is therefore applied to most cases. So, if this term [*innāma*] is mentioned, you should reflect on it. If the context of the text and what is intended indicates delineation of a specific matter, then you should adopt it. Otherwise you should understand the delineation to be absolute. Of this is the saying of the Prophet, may God's blessings and peace be upon him: 'Works are only according to intentions.' What is meant by 'works' here is legally prescribed works. The meaning of the saying is therefore: works are not of any value without the intention, like in the cases of minor ritual ablution (*wuḍū'*), major ritual ablution (*ghusl*), the prayer, the poor-due (*zakāt*), the pilgrimage, and all other acts of worship. As for the removal of impurities, it does not require an intention because it falls under the rubric of abstentions, and an abstention from something does not require an intention. A group of scholars have even stated that both minor and major ritual ablutions without a prior intention are valid.

In the prophetic saying (*works are only according to intention*) there is something omitted (*maḥdhūf*) and the scholars differ in evaluating what is omitted. Those who stipulate the intention as a condition measure the soundness of works through intentions, while those who do not stipulate it as a condition to measure the perfection of works through intentions.

His saying (*and to each person what he intends*) prompted al-Khaṭṭābī to say, 'This points to a particular meaning that is different from the first one, which is specifying work through intention.' Shaykh Muḥyī al-Dīn al-Nawawī said, 'The benefit of mentioning it is that the specification of what is intended is a condition. If a person had to make up prayers, it is not sufficient for him to intend praying missed prayers. Rather, it is a condition that he should intend to pray the Ẓuhr, ʿAṣr or other prayers. Had it not been for the second expression, the first expression would have implied the soundness of making an intention without specification, or it would at least give the impression that the matter is so, and God knows best.'

As for his saying (*whosoever his migration is for God and His Messenger, then his migration is for God and His Messenger*), it is established among the scholars of Arabic that the apodosis and protasis, and the subject of a nominal clause and its predicate must be different. Here, however, they are the same: 'whosoever his migration is for God and His Messenger' by intention and purpose, 'his migration is for God and His Messenger' legally and virtually.

The occasion of this prophetic saying is reported to be a man who migrated from Makkah to Madīnah to marry a woman called Umm Qays, i.e., he did not intend to gain the merit of migration. This man used to be called 'the migrant of Umm Qays', and God knows best.

II

The Elucidation of Islām, Īmān and Iḥsān

عَنْ عُمَرَ رَضِيَ اللَّهُ عَنْهُ أَيْضًا قَالَ: بَيْنَمَا نَحْنُ جُلُوسٌ عِنْدَ رَسُولِ اللَّهِ صَلَّىٰ اللَّهُ عَلَيْهِ وَسَلَّمْ ذَاتَ يَوْمٍ، إِذْ طَلَعَ عَلَيْنَا رَجُلٌ شَدِيدُ بَيَاضِ الثِّيَابِ، شَدِيدُ سَوَادِ الشَّعْرِ، لَا يُرَىٰ عَلَيْهِ أَثَرُ السَّفَرِ، وَلَا يَعْرِفُهُ مِنَّا أَحَدٌ، حَتَّىٰ جَلَسَ إِلَىٰ النَّبِيِّ صَلَّىٰ اللَّهُ عَلَيْهِ وَسَلَّمْ فَأَسْنَدَ رُكْبَتَيْهِ إِلَىٰ رُكْبَتَيْهِ، وَوَضَعَ كَفَّيْهِ عَلَىٰ فَخِذَيْهِ، وَقَالَ: يَا مُحَمَّدُ أَخْبِرْنِي عَنِ الْإِسْلَامِ؟ فَقَالَ رَسُولُ اللَّهِ صَلَّىٰ اللَّهُ عَلَيْهِ وَسَلَّمْ: الْإِسْلَامُ أَنْ تَشْهَدَ أَنْ لَا إِلَٰهَ إِلَّا اللَّهُ وَأَنَّ مُحَمَّدًا رَسُولُ اللَّهِ، وَتُقِيمَ الصَّلَاةَ، وَتُؤْتِيَ الزَّكَاةَ، وَتَصُومَ رَمَضَانَ، وَتَحُجَّ الْبَيْتَ إِنِ اسْتَطَعْتَ إِلَيْهِ سَبِيلًا. قَالَ: صَدَقْتَ. فَعَجِبْنَا لَهُ يَسْأَلُهُ وَيُصَدِّقُهُ. قَالَ: فَأَخْبِرْنِي عَنِ الْإِيمَانِ؟ قَالَ: أَنْ تُؤْمِنَ بِاللَّهِ وَمَلَائِكَتِهِ وَكُتُبِهِ وَرُسُلِهِ وَالْيَوْمِ الْآخِرِ، وَتُؤْمِنَ بِالْقَدَرِ خَيْرِهِ وَشَرِّهِ. قَالَ: صَدَقْتَ.

قَالَ: فَأَخْبِرْنِي عَنِ الْإِحْسَانِ؟ قَالَ: أَنْ تَعْبُدَ اللهَ كَأَنَّكَ تَرَاهُ، فَإِنْ لَمْ تَكُنْ تَرَاهُ فَإِنَّهُ يَرَاكَ. قَالَ: فَأَخْبِرْنِي عَنِ السَّاعَةِ؟ قَالَ: مَا الْمَسْئُولُ عَنْهَا بِأَعْلَمَ مِنَ السَّائِلِ. قَالَ: فَأَخْبِرْنِي عَنْ أَمَارَاتِهَا؟ قَالَ: أَنْ تَلِدَ الْأَمَةُ رَبَّتَهَا، وَأَنْ تَرَى الْحُفَاةَ الْعُرَاةَ الْعَالَةَ رِعَاءَ الشَّاءِ يَتَطَاوَلُونَ فِي الْبُنْيَانِ. ثُمَّ انْطَلَقَ، فَلَبِثْنَا مَلِيًّا، ثُمَّ قَالَ: يَا عُمَرُ أَتَدْرِي مَنِ السَّائِلُ؟ قُلْتُ: اللهُ وَرَسُولُهُ أَعْلَمُ. قَالَ: فَإِنَّهُ جِبْرِيلُ أَتَاكُمْ يُعَلِّمُكُمْ دِينَكُمْ.

رَوَاهُ مُسْلِمٌ [رقم:٨]

It is also reported from ʿUmar, may God be pleased with him, that he said: As we were one day sitting with Allah's Messenger, may God's blessings and peace be upon him, a man came to us. His clothes were extremely white, his hair jet black, and no sign of travelling appeared on him yet none of us knew him. He came towards the Prophet, may Allah's blessings and peace be upon him, sat with his knees touching the Prophet's knees, put his hands on the Prophet's thighs, and then said: 'O Muhammad! Tell me about *Islām*.' God's Messenger, may Allah's blessings and peace be upon him, said: '*Islām* is that you bear witness that there is no deity except Allah and that Muhammad is Allah's Messenger, that you establish the prayer, pay the *zakāt*, fast the month of Ramadan, and make the pilgrimage if you are able to do so.' The man said: 'You have said the truth.' We were all astonished at this man questioning the Prophet and then confirming his answer. Then the man asked: 'Tell me about faith (*Īmān*).' The Prophet said: 'Faith is that you believe in God, His angels, Books, Messengers, the Last Day, and Destiny, its good and its evil.' The man said: 'You have said the truth.' Again he asked: 'Tell me about the state of excellence (*Iḥsān*).' The Prophet said: 'It is to worship God as though you see Him, and, if you do not see Him, He nevertheless sees you.' The man said: 'Tell me about the Last Hour.' The Prophet replied: 'He who is questioned does not know more about it than the questioner does.' The man carried on: 'Tell me then about its signs.' The Prophet said: 'Of its signs is that the slave-woman will give birth to her mistress, and that the naked, barefoot, impoverished ones who graze sheep will build tall buildings.' The man then walked out. We remained there for a while after which the Prophet, may Allah's blessings and peace be upon him, addressed me: 'O ʿUmar! Do you know who the questioner was?' 'God and His Messenger know best', I replied. He said: 'He was the Archangel Gabriel, and he came to teach you your religion.'

This Prophetic saying was narrated by Muslim.

This is a great prophetic saying which comprises all the duties of inward and outward works. The disciplines of the Sacred Law all go back to it, and are in fact derived from it, because it combines all the sciences of the prophetic wont (Sunnah). It is like the mother of the Sunnah just as the opening chapter of the Qur'ān (*al-Fātiḥah*) is the mother of the Qur'ān because it combines all its meanings.

There is evidence in this saying that one must refine one's clothes and appearance and be properly clean when visiting scholars, notables or kings, for Gabriel came to teach people with his state as well as with his words. One of the benefits of this saying is that *Islām* and *Īmān* are two different realities both linguistically and legally. This is the basic rule regarding different names. But the Sacred Law can sometimes be more expansive such that, by way of license, it uses one term to denote another.

His words (*We were all astonished at this man asking the Prophet and then confirming his answer*), i.e., they were astounded because what the Prophet, may God's blessings and peace be upon him, brought is not known except through him. This person, however, was not known to have met the Prophet, may God's blessings and peace be upon him, or to have heard anything from him previously. Moreover, his questioning was that of someone who knew and was certain of the answers, by giving his consent after each response. This is why they were astounded.

His saying (*Faith is that you believe in God, His angels, Books, Messengers, the Last Day, and Destiny, its good and its evil*), i.e., belief in God is the confirmation that God, exalted is He, exists and that He is endowed with the attributes of majesty and beauty, that He is far transcendent above any imperfection, and that He is One, Real, Everlasting, Unique, Creator of all created beings, He disposes with His creation as He wills and does in His kingdom as He wants.

The belief in the angels is to confirm that they are honoured servants who never act without a prior command from God and do what He commands them. The belief in the Messengers of God consists of confirming that they are truthful in what they have reported from God, Most High, that God has supported them with miracles which prove their truthfulness, that they have conveyed from God's messages and explained to those who are legally responsible that which God has commanded them to do, and that it is incumbent to respect these commands and not to make any distinction between them.

The belief in the Last Day is to confirm the Day of Judgement and what it entails of coming back to life after death, the Mustering, the Resurrection, the Reckoning, the Scale, the Bridge over Hell, Paradise and Hell, and that these are His abodes of reward and requital for the righteous and sinners, as well as other auxiliary beliefs that are rigorously authenticated from the prophetic traditions.

Belief in Destiny is the confirmation of all that has been mentioned above. Its gist is what is evidenced from God's saying, *and God created you and what you make* [*al-Ṣāffāt* 37: 96], *Surely We have created everything in measure* [*al-Qamar* 54: 49], and similar verses. Of this is the saying of the Prophet, may God's blessings and peace be upon him, in the tradition related by Ibn ʿAbbās: 'And know that if the nation came together to benefit you with something, they will not be able to do so except with something that God has already destined for you. And if they were to gather to inflict harm on you with something, they will not be able to do so except with something that God has already destined for you. The pens are lifted and the scrolls have dried.'[5]

The doctrine of the pious Predecessors (*salaf*) and the leading scholars who followed them (*khalaf*) is that whoever confirms these beliefs absolutely, without any doubt or hesitation, is truly a believer whether he arrives at these beliefs through categorical proofs or by firm consent.

His saying about excellence, i.e., (*it is to worship God as though you see Him...*) relates to perfecting one's acts of worship, observing the rights of God Most High, being vigilant of Him and summoning His tremendousness and majesty when performing acts of worship.

About his saying (*tell me then about its signs...*), there is a difference of opinion among the scholars regarding the words of the Prophet, may God's blessings and peace be upon him, (*Of its signs is that the slave-woman will give birth to her mistress*). It is said that what is meant is that the Muslims will conquer the lands of the unbelievers and as a consequence taking slave-girls as concubines will be widespread and the children born to these slave-girls from their masters will be like their masters, for their nobility follows from the nobility of their fathers. From this it follows that the capture of the lands of idolaters by the Muslims, abundant conquests and taking slave-girls as concubines are all among the signs of the Last Hour. It is also said that the conditions of people will be so corrupted that the noble among people will sell the mothers of their children and they will be resold again and again to the extent that children may buy their own mothers without realizing. And from this one may conclude that among the signs of the Last Hour is the predominance of ignorance of the fact that such selling is absolutely forbidden. It is also said that it means the widespread lack of dutifulness towards parents among children shall be such that a child will treat his mother like a master treats his slave-girl, by humiliating and cursing her.

(*Impoverished ones*), there is in this saying an indication of the offensiveness (*karāhah*) of what one does not need in terms of constructing buildings and making them quite tall. It is related that the Prophet, may God's blessings and peace be upon him, said: 'The son of Adam will be rewarded for everything except that which he erects on this dust.'[6] The Messenger of God, may God's blessings and peace be upon him, died without edifying his dwelling, expanding it or even embellishing it.

His saying, those (*who graze sheep*), are singled out here because they are the weakest among the dwellers of the desert. And the meaning is: they do so despite their weakness and remoteness from the means leading to such construction, in contrast to the owners of camels who are, on the whole, neither impoverished nor poor.

His saying (*He remained there for a while*) either refers to ʿUmar ibn al-Khaṭṭāb or to the Prophet, may God's blessings and peace be upon him. His saying (*he came to teach you your religion*) means the foundations of your religion or the universals of your religion. This is what Imām al-Nawawī stated in his commentary on this saying included in *Ṣaḥīḥ Muslim*.

The most important thing to mention about this prophetic saying is the exposition of *Islām*, *Īmān* and *Iḥsān* and the obligation to believe by affirming the power of God Almighty. A great deal of things has been said about the explanation of *Islām* and *Īmān*. One of the great scholars who wrote about this is the well-known Mālikī scholar known as Ibn Baṭṭāl who said: 'The doctrine of the group of the people of the Sunnah amongst the pious Predecessors of this community and those who came after them is that faith consists of an utterance and works, and that it grows and decreases due to God's saying, *that they might add faith to their faith* [*al-Fatḥ*48: 4] and other similar verses.' A scholar stated: 'The confirmation in itself does not increase or decrease, but the prescribed faith increases and decreases through the increase or decrease of its fruits which are works.' It is said that there is here reconciliation between the literal meaning of texts which indicate its increase and the original linguistic meaning of the word. And if this opinion is quite obvious, what is more obvious, and Allah knows best, is that the assent itself increases through constant and close scrutiny of the proofs. This is why the faith of those who have assent (*taṣdīq*) is stronger than the faith of others, such that they are not lured by foolishness nor is their faith shaken by any contingency. Rather, their hearts are always joyful and happy regardless of the conditions they go through. As for other than them, they are not the same. This is undeniable. No one doubts that the assent of Abū Bakr al-Ṣiddīq, may God be well pleased with him, is unequalled. This is why Imām Bukhārī has reported in his collection of rigorously authenticated sayings: 'Ibn Abī Malīkah said: "I have met thirty men among the Companions of the Messenger, may God's blessings and peace be upon him, all of whom were afraid of hypocrisy and none of them claimed to have the same faith as Gabriel or Mikā'īl, peace be upon them."'[7] As for using the term faith (*īmān*) to denote works, this is something agreed upon among the people of the truth. The proofs for this are too many to enumerate. God Most High says, *but God would never leave your faith to waste* [*al-Baqarah* 2: 143], i.e., your prayers. It is also related from Shaykh ʿAmr ibn al-Ṣalāḥ regarding the saying of the Prophet, may God's blessings and peace be upon him, that he said: '*Islām* is that you bear witness that there is no god but Allah and that Muhammad is the Messenger of God and that you perform the prayer....' Then he explained faith by saying: 'that you believe in God Most High and His angels...', he said, may God have mercy on him: 'This is the elucidation of the principle of faith, which is the inner assent, and the elucidation of the principle of Islam, which is submission and outward conformity. The ruling of Islam in the outward is affirmed by the two testimonies of faith, the prayer, the poor-due, fasting and the pilgrimage are added to them only because they are the greatest and most manifest rituals of Islam. By performing them one's Islam becomes valid. Moreover, the term faith (*īmān*) includes that by which this prophetic saying and all other acts of obedience are explained because they are the results of the inward assent which is the principle of faith and this is why the designation of "believer" is not given to the person who commits an enormity or abstains from an obligation. For the name of a thing in an absolute manner applies only to that which is perfect and is not used to denote that which is manifestly imperfect except with a certain purpose in doing so. Likewise, it is permissible to deny someone faith, as in the saying of the Prophet, may God's blessings and peace be upon him: "The fornicator does not commit fornication while being a believer and the thief does not commit his theft while being a believer."[8] The term "Islam" also covers the principle of faith which is inward assent, just as it covers the principle of the acts of obedience, for all that amounts to submission.' He went on to add: 'It transpires from what we have mentioned that "*Īmān*" and "*Islām*" have common grounds as well as differences, and that every believer is a Muslim but not every Muslim is a believer. This exposition is likely to reconcile divergent views, and the texts of the Qur'ān and the Sunnah relating to "*Īmān*" and "*Islām*", which have been misunderstood by those who tried to explain them. What we explained agrees with the opinion of the majority of scholars among the practitioners of *Ḥadīth* and others, and God knows best.'

III

The Cardinals of Islam

عَنْ أَبِي عَبْدِ الرَّحْمَنِ عَبْدِ اللهِ بْنِ عُمَرَ بْنِ الْخَطَّابِ رَضِيَ اللهُ عَنْهُمَا قَالَ: سَمِعْتُ رَسُولَ اللهِ صَلَّى اللهُ عَلَيْهِ وَسَلَّمْ يَقُولُ: بُنِيَ الْإِسْلَامُ عَلَى خَمْسٍ: شَهَادَةِ أَنْ لَا إِلَهَ إِلَّا اللهُ وَأَنَّ مُحَمَّدًا رَسُولُ اللهِ، وَإِقَامِ الصَّلَاةِ، وَإِيتَاءِ الزَّكَاةِ، وَحَجِّ الْبَيْتِ، وَصَوْمِ رَمَضَانَ.

رَوَاهُ الْبُخَارِيُّ [رقم:٨] وَمُسْلِمٌ [رقم:١٦]

It is reported from Abū ʿAbd al-Raḥmān ʿAbd Allāh ibn ʿUmar, may God be pleased with both father and son, that he said: I heard God's Messenger, may God's blessings and peace be upon him, say: 'Islam is erected on five cardinals: bearing witness that there is no deity except Allah and that Muhammad is God's Messenger; establishing the prayer; paying the poor-due (*zakāh*); making the pilgrimage; and fasting the days of the month of Ramadan.'

[Narrated by Bukhārī and Muslim]

Abū'l-ʿAbbās al-Qurṭubī, may God be well pleased with him, said: 'This means that these five are the foundations of the religion of Islam, and the pillars upon which it is built and erected. These five were specifically singled out while jihad is not, even though it is by means of it that the religion is made manifest and the stubbornness of the unbelievers is suppressed, is because these five are perpetually obligated whereas jihad is among the collective obligations and is, on some occasions, suspended.'

In some narrated versions of this same prophetic saying the pilgrimage is mentioned before fasting, but this is only due to the narrator's conjecture, and God knows best. This is because when Ibn ʿUmar heard someone repeat this saying by mentioning the pilgrimage before fasting, he rebuked him and told him to mention fasting before the pilgrimage, saying: 'This is how I heard it from the Messenger of God, may God's blessings and peace be upon him.'

In another version related by Ibn ʿUmar, the Prophet, may God's blessings and peace be upon him, said: 'Islam is built upon five things: That you adore God and disbelieve in anything other than Him and that you establish the prayer....'[9] And in another version a man said to ʿAbd Allāh ibn ʿUmar: 'Do you not take part in military conquests?' He said: 'I heard the Messenger of Allah, may God's blessings and peace be upon him, say: "Islam is built upon five...".'

This prophetic saying is a tremendous principle for knowing the religion. One must therefore adopt it for it combines its cardinals.

IV

Works Are Judged by their Ultimate Ends

عَنْ أَبِي عَبْدِ الرَّحْمَنِ عَبْدِ اللَّهِ بْنِ مَسْعُودٍ رَضِيَ اللَّهُ عَنْه قَالَ : حَدَّثَنَا رَسُولُ اللهِ صَلَّىٰ اللَّهُ عَلَيْهِ وَسَلَّمْ - وَهُوَ الصَّادِقُ الْمَصْدُوقُ- : إنَّ أَحدَكُمْ يُجْمعُ خلقُهُ فِي بطْنِ أُمِّهِ أَرْبَعِينَ يوْمًا نُطْفَةً، ثُمَّ يَكُونُ عَلقَةً مِثْلَ ذَلِكَ، ثُمَّ يَكُونُ مُضْغَةً مِثْلَ ذَلِكَ، ثُمَّ يُرْسَلُ إِلَيْهِ الْمَلَكُ فَيَنْفُخُ فِيهِ الرُّوحَ، وَيُؤْمَرُ بِأَرْبَعِ كَلِماتٍ: بِكَتْبِ رِزْقِهِ، وَأَجَلِهِ، وَعَمَلِهِ، وَشَقِيٌّ أَوْ سَعِيدٌ. فَوَاللهِ الَّذِي لَا إِلَهَ غَيْرُهُ إنَّ أَحَدَكُمْ ليَعْمَلُ بِعَمَلِ أَهْلِ الْجَنَّةِ حَتَّىٰ مَا يَكُونُ بَيْنَهُ وَبَيْنَهَا إِلَّا ذِرَاعٌ فَيَسْبِقُ عَلَيْهِ الْكِتَابُ فَيَعْمَلُ بِعَمَلِ أَهْلِ النَّارِ فَيَدْخُلُهَا. وَإِنَّ أَحَدَكُمْ لَيَعْمَلُ بِعَمَلِ أَهْلِ النَّارِ حَتَّىٰ مَا يَكُونُ بَيْنَهُ وَبَيْنَهَا إِلَّا ذِرَاعٌ فَيَسْبِقُ عَلَيْهِ الْكِتَابُ فَيَعْمَلُ بِعَمَلِ أَهْلِ الْجَنَّةِ فَيَدْخُلُهَا.

رَوَاهُ الْبُخَارِيُّ [رقم:٣٢٠٨] وَمُسْلِمٌ [رقم:٢٦٤٣]

It is reported that Abū ʿAbd al-Raḥmān ʿAbd Allāh ibn Masʿūd, may God be pleased with him, said: Allah's Messenger, may God be pleased with him, who is most truthful and credible, said to us: 'The stuff from which each person is created is gathered in his mother's womb as a sperm for forty days, then as a blood clot for the same period, then as a lump of flesh for the same period. Upon which an angel is sent to breathe the spirit into him, and the angel is commanded with four matters: to record his sustenance, death, works and whether he is saved or damned. By Him Who is the only God! One of you would observe the works of the people of Paradise until there is only a cubit between him and Paradise, but then the Register would forestall him and he would perform an act of the people of Hellfire and consequently enters it. And one of you would observe the works of the people of Hellfire until there is only a cubit between him and it, but then the Register would forestall him and he would perform an act of the people of Paradise and consequently enters it.'

[Narrated by Bukhārī and Muslim]

A scholar said: 'The meaning of his saying (*The stuff from which each person is created is gathered in his mother's womb as a sperm...*) is that semen falls scattered in the womb and so God gathers it at the place of birth inside the womb during this time. His words (*Upon which an angel is sent...*) means the angel entrusted with the womb.

It seems from the literal meaning of this prophetic saying (*One of you would observe the works of the people of Paradise...*) that the works of such a person are valid and that he draws closer to Paradise due to his works until there is nothing between him and entering it except the distance of a cubit. What prevents him from entering it though is what is pre-eternally decreed, and this is only revealed at his ultimate end. Hence works are but according to what has been pre-eternally decreed. But because what has been pre-eternally decreed is veiled from us and the ultimate end is manifest, it is mentioned in the prophetic saying (*Works are judged but by the ultimate ends*), i.e., as far as we are concerned in relation to our knowledge of some people and only in some occasions. As for the prophetic saying narrated by Muslim in his rigorously-authenticated collection, in the Book of Faith, that the Messenger of God, may God's blessings and peace be upon him, said: 'A man performs the works of the people of Paradise in appearance while being of the denizens of Hell', this person's works are not valid in themselves due to being tainted with showing off and longing to gain a reputation among people. The conclusion that one draws from this prophetic saying is that one must not rely on works but rather on God's generosity and mercy, and God knows best.

By his saying (*By Him Who is the only God! One of you would observe the works of the people of Paradise until...*) is meant that this happens on rare occasions, not that it happens to most people. This is due to God's subtle kindness and abundant mercy, for it is very frequent that people turn away from evil to good while their turning away from good to evil is extremely rare, by God's praise and grace. This prophetic saying affirms the Decree in the doctrine of the people of the Sunnah that all events are by God's decree and destiny, the good and the bad, the beneficial as well as the harmful. God Most High says: *He shall not be questioned as to what He does, but they shall be questioned* [*al-Anbiyā'* 21: 23]. It also illustrates that there is no objection to God in His Kingdom: He does in His kingdom what He wills. Imām Samʿānī said: 'The way to know this rubric is to combine the Qur'ān and the Sunnah and leave out pure analogy and abstract reasoning. Whoever fails to combine the texts of the Qur'ān and the Sunnah will be misguided and lost in the abyss of bewilderment. He will never attain to that which satisfies the soul nor find tranquillity of heart. This is because the Decree is of the secrets of God Most High, which is concealed by many veils: God kept its secret to Himself and concealed it from the minds of people. God has concealed the knowledge of the Decree from the world such that no angel or prophet who has been sent knows it. It is also said: "The secret of the Decree will be revealed to people once they enter Paradise, and not before that."'

There are many prophetic traditions that warn against leaving works in submission to what has been pre-eternally ordained. Rather, works and legal prescriptions are incumbent when the Sacred Law commands them. And every person is helped to fulfil what he has been created for, as he cannot do other than that. As for the person who is among the saved, God will make it easy for him to perform the works of those who attain salvation. And as for the person who is among the damned, God will make it easy for him to do the works of those who are damned, as mentioned in the prophetic saying. God Most High also says: *But as for him who is a miser and is self-sufficient, and cries lies to the reward most fair, We shall surely ease him to the Hardship; his wealth shall not avail him when he persihes* [*al-Layl* 92: 7–10]. The scholars have stated: 'The Book of God, His Tablet, and the Pen are things that one is obligated to believe in. As for what the Tablet and the Pen are or their description, only God knows, for they do not encompass anything of His knowledge except as He wills, and God knows best.

V

The Nullity of Repulsive and Blameworthy Innovations

عَـنْ أُمِّ الْمُؤْمِنِينَ أُمِّ عَبْدِ اللهِ عَائِشَةَ رَضِيَ اللهُ عَنْهَا، قَالَتْ: قَالَ: رَسُولُ اللهِ صَلَّى اللهُ عَلَيْهِ وَسَلَّمَ: مَنْ أَحْدَثَ فِي أَمْرِنَا هَذَا مَا لَيْسَ مِنْهُ فَهُوَ رَدٌّ.

رَوَاهُ الْبُخَارِيُّ [رقم:٢٦٩٧] وَمُسْلِمٌ [رقم:١٧١٨]

وَفِي رِوَايَةٍ لِمُسْلِمٍ: مَنْ عَمِلَ عَمَلًا لَيْسَ عَلَيْهِ أَمْرُنَا فَهُوَ رَدٌّ.

It is related that that the mother of the believers Umm ʿAbd Allāh ʿĀ'ishah, may Allah be well pleased with her, said: Allah's Messenger, may Allah's blessings and peace be upon him, said: 'Whosoever brings any new matter into this religion of ours without any basis, it shall be categorically rejected.'

[Narrated by Bukhārī and Muslim]; and in another narration of Mulim's: 'Whosoever performs an act which is not in accordance with our matter, it shall be categorically rejected.'

His saying (*is not according to our matter*) means 'is not according to our judgement'. This prophetic saying is one of the most tremendous foundations of the religion. It is also an example of the Prophet's most concise and comprehensive speech, may God's blessings and peace be upon him. This is because it is absolutely clear in its rebuttal of blameworthy innovations and of any newly-begun matters. It is also an evidence for the vitiation of all forbidden contracts and the inexistence of their consequences. Some scholars of legal theory used this saying as proof that the prohibition here entails nullity.

The other version in which the Prophet, may God's blessings and peace be upon him, said: 'Whoever performs a work which does not conform to our matter is absolutely rejected' is very clear in the necessity of leaving all newly- begun matters, whether the matter is begun by the person himself or by someone else before him. This is because, upon performing a blameworthy innovation, an obstinate person may say: 'I have not innovated anything' and so this second version will be used as evidence against him.

There are also things in this saying that deserve to be kept in mind, propagated to others and used to invalidate all repulsive matters, for it deals with all of that. As for deducting principles that do not clash with the Sunnah, this absolute rejection does not address it. An example of the latter is the writing of the Noble Qur'ān in the form of one book, the legal schools which are the fruits of close research by the highest calibre of jurists who measure the auxiliary matters of law with the principles, i.e., the words of the Messenger of God, may God's blessings and peace be upon him, or such as the books authored on grammar, calculus and the shares of inheritance, as well as other disciplines whose point of reference and contents are the words and commands of the Messenger of God, may God's blessings and peace be upon him. All of this is not included in the absolute rejection referred to in the above prophetic saying.

VI

The Lawful is Clearly Evident and the Unlawful is Clearly Evident

عَنْ أَبِي عَبْدِ اللهِ النُّعْمَانِ بْنِ بَشِيرٍ رَضِيَ اللهُ عَنْهُمَا، قَالَ: سَمِعْتُ رَسُولَ اللهِ صَلَّىٰ اللهُ عَلَيْهِ وَسَلَّمَ يَقُولُ: إِنَّ الْحَلَالَ بَيِّنٌ، وَإِنَّ الْحَرَامَ بَيِّنٌ، وَبَيْنَهُمَا أُمُورٌ مُشْتَبِهَاتٌ لَا يَعْلَمُهُنَّ كَثِيرٌ مِنْ النَّاسِ، فَمَنْ اتَّقَىٰ الشُّبُهَاتِ فَقَدْ اسْتَبْرَأَ لِدِينِهِ وَعِرْضِهِ، وَمَنْ وَقَعَ فِي الشُّبُهَاتِ وَقَعَ فِي الْحَرَامِ، كَالرَّاعِي يَرْعَىٰ حَوْلَ الْحِمَىٰ يُوشِكُ أَنْ يَرْتَعَ فِيهِ، أَلَا وَإِنَّ لِكُلِّ مَلِكٍ حِمًى، أَلَا وَإِنَّ حِمَىٰ اللهِ مَحَارِمُهُ، أَلَا وَإِنَّ فِي الْجَسَدِ مُضْغَةً إِذَا صَلَحَتْ صَلَحَ الْجَسَدُ كُلُّهُ، وَإِذَا فَسَدَتْ فَسَدَ الْجَسَدُ كُلُّهُ، أَلَا وَهِيَ الْقَلْبُ.

رَوَاهُ الْبُخَارِيُّ [رقم:٥٢]، وَمُسْلِمٌ [رقم:١٥٩٩]

On the authority of ʿAbd Allāh al-Nuʿmān ibn Bashīr, may Allah be well pleased with him, who said: I heard Allah's Messenger, may Allah's blessings and peace be upon him, saying: 'The lawful is clearly evident and the unlawful is clearly evident too, and between the two exist ambiguous matters that many people do not know about. Whosoever avoids these ambiguous matters has exonerated his religion and honour, and whosoever falls into them has fallen into the unlawful. The latter is like a shepherd who pastures around a preserve and is on the verge of violating it. Verily, each king has a preserve, and God's preserve is His prohibitions. Verily, there is in the body a chunk of meat, which when it is sound the whole body is sound, and when it is corrupted the whole body is corrupted. This chunk of meat is the heart.'

[Narrated by Bukhārī and Muslim]

This prophetic saying is also a great principle in the Sacred Law. Abū Dāwūd al-Sijistānī mentioned that Islam revolves around four prophetic sayings, and he mentioned this saying among them. The scholars of Islam are unanimous about its great eminence and abundant benefits.

His saying (*The lawful is clearly evident...*) means that matters are divided into three categories: (i) Those [matters] whose lawfulness is stated by God to be lawful, such as His saying Most High, *Today the good things are permitted you, and the food of those who were given the Book is permitted to you* [*al-Māʾidah* 5: 5], His saying, *Lawful for you, beyond all that* [*al-Nisāʾ* 4: 24], and similar other verses. (ii) Those [matters] whose unlawfulness is stated by God to be clearly unlawful, such as His saying, *Forbidden to you are your mothers and daughters* [*al-Nisāʾ* 4: 23], *but forbidden to you is the game of the land, so long as you remain in pilgrim sanctity* [*al-Māʾidah* 5: 96], and the prohibition of manifest and hidden vile deeds. Anything upon which God has placed a fixed, legal punishment, a punitive measure or a threat is unlawful. (iii) As for ambiguous matters, they are those that are disputed according to the evidences of the Qur'ān and the Sunnah. Refraining from such matters is therefore a sign of scrupulousness.

Muslim scholars have differed about the legal ruling of these ambiguous matters alluded to by the Prophet, may God's blessings and peace be upon him, in this saying. Some are of the opinion that they are unlawful due to his word, may God's blessings and peace be upon him, 'Whosoever avoids these ambiguous matters has exonerated his religion and honour' for, according to them, whoever does not exonerate his religion and honour has fallen into the unlawful. Other scholars are of the opinion that they are lawful and the proof for this is the words of the Prophet, may God's blessings and peace be upon him, in the same saying: 'the latter is like a shepherd...', which indicates its lawfulness even though leaving it points to one's scrupulousness. Yet another group of scholars maintained that the ambiguous matters mentioned in this saying cannot be said to be either lawful or unlawful, for they are placed between the clearly lawful and the clearly unlawful. It is therefore incumbent that one remains undecided about them out of scrupulousness.

It is also well established from the prophetic saying narrated in the rigorously-authenticated collections of Bukhārī and Muslim on the authority of ʿĀ'ishah, may God be well pleased with her, that she said: 'Saʿd ibn Abī Waqqāṣ and ʿAbd ibn Zumʿah went to the Messenger of Allah, may God's blessings and peace be upon him, to settle a dispute they had about a boy. The former said: "O Messenger of God! This is the son of my brother ʿUtbah ibn Abī Waqqāṣ. He left him with us to look after as his son. Just look at the resemblance between them." ʿAbd ibn Zumʿah said: "This is my brother, O Messenger of God! He was born in my father's bed from his slave-girl." The Messenger of God, may God's blessings and peace be upon him, looked at the boy and noticed a clear resemblance to ʿUtbah. He therefore said: "The boy is yours, O Zumʿah! A child is attributed to the person to whom it is born, while the fornicator has nothing but disappointment. You have to keep out of his view, O Sawdah!"'[10] And so Sawdah never saw him. The Messenger of Allah, may God's blessings and peace be upon him, decreed that the child is attributed to the man it is born to and that it belonged, on the face of it, to Zumʿah and that he is the brother of Sawdah, the wife of the Prophet, may God's blessings and peace be upon him, by way of likelihood, not that the matter was categorically clear. Then he ordered Sawdah to keep out of view from him due to the doubt arising from the lack of certitude about his father. He thus took the path of precaution, which is the wont of those who fear God, exalted is He. For if the child belonged to Ibn Zumʿah in God's knowledge, he would not have asked his wife to keep out of his view, just as he did not command her to do so with her other brothers, slaves or otherwise.

And in the prophetic saying relating to ʿAdī ibn Ḥātim, he said: 'O Messenger of God! I unleash my dog and pronounce the *basmalah* on him, but it happens that I find my dog with the game caught by another dog.' The Messenger of God, may God's blessings and peace be upon him, said: 'Do not consume it, for you have pronounced the *basmalah* on your dog, not the other one.'[11] And so the Messenger, may God's blessings and peace be upon him, declared that it was an ambiguous matter and that the game was as if it had been offered to other than God, when God Most High has said, *it is ungodliness* [*al-Anʿām* 6: 121]. Therefore, there is in the edict of the Prophet, may God's blessings and peace be upon him, an indication for one to be cautious in events and eventualities that have the potential to be either lawful or unlawful due to the resemblance of their causes. This is the meaning of the saying of the Prophet, may God's blessings and peace be upon him: 'Leave that about which you are in doubt for that which you are not.'[12]

A scholar said: 'Ambiguous matters are of three categories: there are those matters which the person knows are unlawful but is in doubt about whether their unlawfulness is still applicable or not. An example of this is what is unlawful for a person to eat before lawful slaughtering. If a person doubts that the animal is slaughtered, the latter's unlawfulness is not vitiated until he is certain of its lawful slaughter. The point of reference for such a position is the above-mentioned saying related by ʿAdī.

'The second category, by contrast, includes those matters that a person knows are lawful but is in doubt about their unlawfulness. An example of this is a married man who doubts whether or not he divorced his wife, or a person who has a slave-girl and is in doubt about her manumission. Matters of this category are to be taken as lawful until one finds out that they are otherwise. The evidence for this finds support in the saying related by ʿAbd Allāh ibn Zayd[13] about the person who doubts whether or not he has vitiated his ritual purity after being certain of being in a state of ritual purity.

'The third category is for a person to have doubt about whether something is lawful or unlawful, with the possibility of its being either and there is no indication to suggest either its lawfulness or unlawfulness. The best course of action in this case is to adopt the way of caution and to consider it unlawful, just as the Prophet, may God's blessings and peace be upon him, did when he found a date that had fallen in his house, saying: "I would have eaten it if I did not fear that it might belong to the dates given in charity."'[14]

As for opting for the opposite, such as in the case when a matter is preponderantly lawful because of an imagined reason that has no basis, like abstaining from using unchanged water out of fear that some impurity might have fallen in it, or refusing to pray in a spot without any trace of impurity out of fear that it contains urine that has dried, or washing one's clothes out of fear that any impurity might have touched them – these kinds of things should not be considered at all. This is because remaining undecided in such cases amounts to nothing but delusion and any imagined scrupulousness in them is but the Devil's intimations for there is nothing doubtful or ambiguous about them.

His saying (*that many people do not know*), i.e., they do not know their legal rulings, whether they are lawful or not. Otherwise, the person who knows of an ambiguous matter knows it to be a problematic question that is likely to be any one thing among many probabilities. So when he knows to which principle it is to be annexed, it no longer remains an ambiguous matter and becomes either lawful or unlawful. There is here also a proof that an ambiguous matter has a specific ruling which is backed by legal evidence that some people may reach.

His saying (*and whosoever falls into them has fallen into the unlawful*) can take place in two ways: the first being that whoever does not fear God and dares to engage in ambiguous matters will inevitably end up engaging in prohibited matters. His carelessness in engaging in ambiguous matters will lead him to engage daringly in that which is unlawful. One scholar said: 'A small sin may lead to a major one, and a major sin may lead to unbelief.' And as it is related: 'Contraventions are the smooth pathways to disbelief.'

The second is that whoever engages frequently in ambiguous matters, his heart will be darkened due to its being deprived of the light of knowledge and the light of scrupulousness. And because of this he will fall unaware into that which is unlawful, in which case he might be sinful if this results in negligence.

His saying (*like a shepherd...*) is a simile struck to explain the limits set by God. The Arabs used to delineate preserves to protect their cattle and would threaten anyone who dared to go close to them. The person who is afraid of the punishment of the king will keep his cattle away from that preserve, for, if he goes close to it, it is very likely that he will violate it, as any sheep could leave its flock and walk into it. The precaution to take, therefore, is to keep at a safe distance from the preserve. The same applies to God's set limits, such as murder, usury, theft, consuming intoxicants, slander, backbiting, tale-bearing and other similar sins. This is why one should not come close to them out of fear of falling into them.

His saying (*Verily, there is in the body a chunk of meat...*) [refers to] the heart, the noblest of all faculties because it is the locus of swift, recurrent thoughts. God Most High has given this faculty specifically to the animal species and deposited in it the ability to regulate intended benefits. One finds that all kinds of beasts apprehend, through this faculty, their benefits and distinguish what is harmful to them. God has then specifically given human beings reason in addition to the faculty of heart, and so He said: *What, have they not journeyed in the land so that they have hearts to understand with or ears to hear with?* [*al-Ḥajj* 22: 46].

God has made the limbs subservient to the heart, whatever falls into the heart will be manifest on the limbs by them acting on its effect. If the effect is good, then the action will be good; if it is bad, then the action will be bad. If one understands this, one can understand the words of the Messenger of God, 'Verily there is in the body....' We ask God Almighty to correct the corruption of our hearts. O Changer of hearts! Make our hearts firm in Your religion. O Disposer of hearts! Dispose our hearts to Your obedience.

VII

Religion is Doing Well by Others

عَنْ أَبِي رُقَيَّةَ تَمِيمِ بْنِ أَوْسٍ الدَّارِيِّ رَضِيَ اللهُ عَنْهُ أَنَّ النَّبِيَّ صَلَّى اللهُ عَلَيْهِ وَسَلَّمْ قَالَ: الدِّينُ النَّصِيحَةُ. قُلْنَا: لِمَنْ؟ قَالَ: لِلَّهِ، وَلِكِتَابِهِ، وَلِرَسُولِهِ، وَلِأَئِمَّةِ الْمُسْلِمِينَ وَعَامَّتِهِمْ.

رَوَاهُ مُسْلِمٌ [رقم: ٥٥]

On the authority of Abū Ruqayyah Tamīm ibn Aws al-Dārī, may Allah be well pleased with him, that the Prophet, may Allah's blessings and peace be upon him, said: 'Religion is doing well by others.' We said: 'Doing well by whom, O Messenger of Allah?' He said: 'By God, His Book, His Messenger, as well as by the leaders of the Muslims and by their commonality.'

[Narrated by Muslim]

Tamīm al-Dārī, may God be well pleased with him, has not related anything except this prophetic saying. '*Naṣīḥah*' [which is translated here as 'doing well by others'] is a comprehensive term that denotes the willingness of a sum of good measures or instructions for the benefit or the sake of the person that one would like to do well by. It is a concise and pregnant word. In fact, the Arabs do not possess a single word that conveys the meaning of this word. Like they said about the word *falāḥ*: 'There is nothing in the speech of the Arabs that combines the good of this world and of the next better than it.'

The meaning of his saying (*Religion is doing well by others*) is that doing well by others is its pillar and what it stands on, like his saying: 'The pilgrimage is ʿArafah',[15] i.e., its main component and cardinal.

As for the explanation of doing well by others (*naṣīḥah*) and its different sub-categories, al-Khaṭṭābī and other scholars said: 'The meaning of doing well by God Most High relates to having faith in Him, rejecting associating others with Him and abstaining from attributing any unbecoming trait to His attributes. He must be described by all the attributes of perfection and majesty and exonerated from all imperfections. One must obey Him and shun His disobedience; love for His sake and hate for His sake. One must fight against those who disbelieve in Him and acknowledge His blessings and give thanks for them. One must also have sincerity in all matters, prompt people to have the same and be gentle in the treatment of people.' Al-Khaṭṭābī added: 'The reality of these traits relates to the servant himself upon doing well by himself, for God Most High is exalted above the need of requiring being well done to by anyone.'

As for doing well by the Book of God Most High, it is that one believes that it is God's speech and His Revealed Words, that it does not resemble the speech of humans and that no created being can produce something like it. One must also exalt it and recite it as it should be recited, according to the rules of recitation and with humility. One must also defend it against the interpretations of distorters, believe in its content and comply with its rulings. One must understand its disciplines and similes, take heed of its passages, meditate on its wonders, act upon that which is unambiguous (*muḥkam*) in it, submit to that which is ambiguous (*mutashābih*), look for that which is of general applicability in it, call for it as well as for that which we have mentioned of its counsels.

As for doing well by the Messenger of God, may God's blessings and peace be upon him, it is to accept his message, believe in everything he brought, obey him in his commands and prohibitions, vindicate him whether in his life or after his death, show enmity towards anyone who declares enmity towards him, ally oneself with whoever allies himself with him, exalt his right and venerate him, revive his wont and way, respond to his call, propagate his Sunnah and defend it against any attack, prefer the study of its sciences and gain understanding of its meaning. One must also call for his Sunnah, be gentle in teaching, exalting and glorifying it, show proper decorum when reading it and abstain from talking about it without knowledge. One must also show respect towards its folk because of their connection to it. One must assume his character traits, embody his manners, love the members of his household and his Companions and shun whoever initiates blameworthy innovations in his Sunnah or speaks ill of his Companions.

As for doing well by the leaders of the Muslims, it consists of helping them to establish what is right, obeying them, commanding them to establish what is right, exhorting and reminding them with gentleness and kindness. One must inform them about that which they have become oblivious to, convey to them what rights are due to Muslims, avoid violent rebellion against them, reconcile people's hearts to obey and pray behind them, take part in jihad with them, and pray for them to have righteousness.

As for doing well by the commonality of Muslims, i.e., other than the rulers, it is to guide them towards their own interests in the world to come and in this world, help them to achieve these benefits, conceal their faults, fulfil their needs, drive away harm from them and bring about benefits for them. One must also enjoin them to do good and forbid them from engaging in evil with sincerity and gentleness. One must show pity towards them, respect the old amongst them, show mercy towards the young among them and never fail to exhort them well. One must abstain from cheating them or displaying resentful envy towards them. One must love for them what one loves for oneself of the good, and dislike for them what one dislikes for oneself of disliked things. One must defend their property, honour and other things relating to them through actions and words. One must also encourage them to embody all what we have mentioned of the different kinds of doing well by, and God knows best.

Doing well by others is a collective obligation (*farḍ kifāyah*), and if it is sufficiently established by some, then the obligation of fulfilling it is no longer incumbent upon the rest.

The Inviolability of
the Muslim

عَـنْ ابْنِ عُمَرَ رَضِيَ اللَّهُ عَنْهُمَا، أَنَّ رَسُوْلَ اللَّهِ صَلَّى اللَّهُ عَلَيْهِ
وَسَلَّمَ قَالَ: أُمِرْتُ أَنْ أُقَاتِلَ النَّاسَ حَتَّى يَشْهَدُوا أَنْ لَا إِلَهَ
إِلَّا اللَّهُ وَأَنَّ مُحَمَّدًا رَسُوْلُ اللَّهِ، وَيُقِيْمُوا الصَّلَاةَ، وَيُؤْتُوا
الزَّكَاةَ فَإِذَا فَعَلُوا ذَلِكَ عَصَمُوا مِنِّي دِمَاءَهُمْ وَأَمْوَالَهُمْ إِلَّا بِحَقِّ
الْإِسْلَامِ، وَحِسَابُهُمْ عَلَى اللَّهِ تَعَالَى.

رَوَاهُ الْبُخَارِيُّ [رقم:٢٥] وَمُسْلِمٌ [رقم:٢٢]

On the authority of Ibn ʿUmar, may God be well pleased with
him, who reported that the Messenger of God, may God's blessings and peace be upon him, said: 'I was commanded to fight
people until they bear witness that there is no god except God
and that Muhammad is God's Messenger, establish the prayer
and pay the poor-due. If they do this, their lives and properties
become inviolable with me unless it be by the right of Islam, and
their reckoning is with God.'

[Narrated by Bukhārī and Muslim]

This is a tremendous saying and one of the foundations of the religion. The version related by Anas has: 'Until they bear witness that there is no god except God and that Muhammad is His servant and Messenger and that they pray facing towards our direction of prayer (*qiblah*), eat our slaughtered animals and perform our prayers. If they do so their lives and properties become inviolable for us except if a right is due on the same; they shall enjoy the same rights the Muslims have and discharge the same duties that the Muslims do.'[16] And in the version narrated by Muslim in his collection on the authority of Abū Hurayrah: 'until they bear witness that there is no god except God, believe in me and in that which I have brought', the meaning of which conforms to the version reported by Ibn ʿUmar.

As for the meaning of this saying, the scholars of international Islamic law (*siyar*) say: 'When the Messenger of God, may God's blessings and peace be upon him, died and was succeeded by Abū Bakr al-Ṣiddīq, may God be well pleased with him, as the leader of the Muslim community, some of the Arabs became apostates, whereas some refused to pay the poor-due due to their own interpretation of this obligation without abandoning Islam altogether. Abū Bakr al-Ṣiddīq decided to fight both. But ʿUmar ibn al-Khaṭṭāb objected, saying: "How can you fight people who say 'There is no god but God' when the Messenger of God, may God's blessings and peace be upon him, has said: 'I was commanded to fight people until they say: 'there is no god but God....'" Abū Bakr al-Ṣiddīq replied: "The poor-due is the right due on wealth. By God! If they withhold from me a she-kid (and in another version: a cord used for hobbling the feet of camels) – which they used to pay to the Messenger of God, may God's blessings and peace be upon him – I would fight them for it", after which ʿUmar went along with him in fighting those people.'

Regarding his saying (*I was commanded to fight people until they bear witness that there is no god except God and that Muhammad is God's Messenger*), al-Khaṭṭābī said concerning this: 'Those meant by this are the worshippers of idols and Arab idolaters and those who refuse to believe; the people of the Book are not included in this.'

But to pronounce the oneness of God is not enough to secure the inviolability of a person's life and wealth, i.e., if he says it with his tongue while still harbouring unbelief in his heart. It is mentioned in another prophetic saying: 'And that I am indeed the Messenger of God, and that they establish the prayer and pay the poor-due.' Shaykh Muḥyī al-Dīn al-Nawawī said: 'Despite this, it is still incumbent to believe in everything brought by the Messenger of God, may God's blessings and peace be upon him, as in the other version reported by Abū Hurayrah: 'until they bear witness that there is no god except God and believe in me and in that which I have brought.'[17]

(*Their reckoning is with God*), i.e., regarding that which they hide and keep concealed, not that which they fail to perform outwardly of the obligated prescriptions. Al-Khaṭṭābī mentioned this and said: 'One deduces from this that the person who manifests his adherence to Islam but conceals his disbelief, his outward acceptance of Islam is accepted.' This is the opinion of the majority of scholars. Imām Mālik on the other hand is of the opinion that the repentance of someone who professes outwardly the opposite of what he believes inwardly (*zindīq*) is not accepted; this is also one of the opinions attributed to Imām Aḥmad.

In his saying (*I was commanded to fight people until they bear witness that there is no god but God and believe in me and in that which I have brought*), there is a clear indication of the doctrine of the greatest of the scholars as well as of the majority among the pious Predecessors and those who came after them which states that if a person believes firmly and unwaveringly in Islam, this should be sufficient for him and he does not have to learn the proof of the speculative theologians to know God through them, contrary to those who have made the knowledge of such proofs incumbent to guarantee the safety of those who believe in Islam. The latter opinion is clearly wrong for what is sought in the matter is firm assent, and this has already happened. Moreover, the Prophet, may God's blessings and peace be upon him, confined his words to having assent in that which he brought and did not make knowledge with proof a condition for it. A number of other prophetic traditions in the rigorously-authenticated collections support this thesis. Taking all these traditions together conveys mass transmission of this prophetic saying as well as categorical knowledge, and God knows best.

IX

Charging People With Only What They Can Bear

عَنْ أَبِي هُرَيْرَةَ عَبْدِ الرَّحْمَنِ بْنِ صَخْرٍ رَضِيَ اللهُ عَنْهُ قَالَ: سَمِعْتُ رَسُولَ اللهِ صَلَّى اللهُ عَلَيْهِ وَسَلَّمَ يَقُولُ: مَا نَهَيْتُكُمْ عَنْهُ فَاجْتَنِبُوهُ، وَمَا أَمَرْتُكُمْ بِهِ فَأْتُوا مِنْهُ مَا اسْتَطَعْتُمْ، فَإِنَّمَا أَهْلَكَ الَّذِينَ مِنْ قَبْلِكُمْ كَثْرَةُ مَسَائِلِهِمْ وَاخْتِلَافُهُمْ عَلَى أَنْبِيَائِهِمْ.

رَوَاهُ الْبُخَارِيُّ [رقم:٧٢٨٨] وَمُسْلِمٌ [رقم:١٣٣٧]

On the authority of Abū Hurayrah ʿAbd al-Raḥmān ibn Ṣakhr, may God be well pleased with him, who said: I heard the Messenger of God, may God's blessings and peace be upon him, say: 'That which I warned you against, avoid it, and that which I commanded you to do, do it to the best of your ability. Indeed, what has destroyed people before you is their abundant questioning of and opposition to their prophets.'

[Narrated by Bukhārī and Muslim]

The wording of this saying in the collection of Muslim as reported on the authority of Abū Hurayrah is: 'The Messenger of God, may God's blessings and peace be upon him, exhorted us saying: "O people! God has made the pilgrimage obligatory on you, so do perform the pilgrimage." A man asked: "Should it be every year, O Messenger of God?" But the Messenger, may God's blessings and peace be upon him, kept silent. The man repeated his question three times, upon which the Messenger of God, may God's blessings and peace be upon him, said: "It would have become obligatory on you if I had said 'yes' and you would not have been able to perform it every year." Then he said: "Leave me as long as I leave you, for indeed what has destroyed the people before you is their abundant questioning of and opposition to their prophets. So when I command you with something, do it to the best of your ability, and when I warn you against something, you should avoid it."' The man who asked the question is al-Aqraᶜ ibn Ḥābis, as shown in a different narration of this prophetic saying.

Legal theorists have differed about this matter, i.e., whether the repetition of the obligation is incumbent or not? Most jurists and theologians are of the opinion that it is not. Others, however, are of the opinion that one cannot rule either that it is obligatory every year or non-obligatory. Rather, anything exceeding the first performance should be subject to more explanation.

This prophetic saying could be used as evidence by those who declare themselves undecided in this matter, for the man asked: 'Is it every year?' Had the absolute terms of the *ḥadīth* implied repetition or non-repetition, the Prophet, may God's blessings and peace be upon him, would not have said: 'It would have been made incumbent on you if I had said "yes".' In fact, there would not have been any need to ask, as its face value indicates it. The Muslim community is unanimous that the pilgrimage is obligatory just once in one's lifetime according to Islamic Sacred Law.

As for his saying (*Leave me alone for as long as I leave you alone*), it clearly shows that the matter does require repetition, and it also indicates that the initial ruling is the non-obligation of repetition and that there is no legal ruling before the advent of the Sacred Law, which is the correct position among numerous legal theorists.

His saying (*It would have been made incumbent on you had I said 'yes'*) is proof for the correct opinion, which states that the Prophet, may God's blessings and peace be upon him, had the authority to make *ijtihād* regarding legal rulings, and that it is not a condition that his ruling must be through revelation.

His words (*that which I commanded you to do, do it to the best of your ability*) contain one of the most important rules of Islam and are an example of his comprehensive speech, may God's blessings and peace be upon him. The legal rulings that come under this rule are beyond count, such as the prayer when the praying person is unable to perform some of its cardinals or conditions. What the person has to do in such a case is to perform the rest of the prayer that he can perform. Likewise, when a person is unable to wash some of his limbs in ritual ablution, he washes those parts that he can wash. The same applies to when the *zakāt al-fiṭr* of the group of people one is obliged to spend on becomes obligatory or when it comes to removing objectionable matters if one cannot remove all of them, in both cases the person does what he is able to do. There are also innumerable similar questions that are well known in the books of jurisprudence. This prophetic saying conveys the same meaning as the words of God

Most High, *So fear God as far as you are able* [*al-Taghābun* 64: 16]. As for His words, *O believers, fear God as He should be feared* [*Āl ʿImrān* 3: 102] it is said that it is abrogated by His words, *So fear God as far as you are able*. A scholar said: 'The correct position is that it is not abrogated by this verse. Rather, this verse further explains the other verse and what is meant by it.' Some scholars stated that *as He should be feared* (*ḥaqqa tuqātih*) is tantamount to complying with His commands and avoiding His prohibitions. God has not commanded except that which is within the ability of people, for God Most High says, *God charges no soul save to its capacity* [*al-Baqarah* 2: 286], *and has laid on you no impediment in your religion* [*al-Ḥajj* 22: 78].

As for his saying, may God's blessings and peace be upon him, (*and that which I have warned you against, avoid it*), this is absolutely the case. However, when there is an excuse that renders it permissible, such as eating the flesh of dead animals out of necessity and in similar cases, the matter is not prohibited in such conditions. Other than where there is an excuse, one would not be complying with the implication of prohibition until one refrains from everything that is prohibited without exception, and does not fail to do so in contravening even a single command. When this principle is understood, it is a question of command in an absolute sense, but does one understand from it that the execution of the command should be immediate? Or is a degree of delay allowed? Does it refer to one instance of executing an order or to its repetition? Hence, in this prophetic saying, there are many rubrics of Islamic jurisprudence, and God knows best.

His saying (*Verily, what has destroyed nations before you...*) after saying (*leave me alone for as long as I leave you alone*) means: Do not ask too many questions, for it may well happen that the answers will come in abundance such that you become like the Children of Israel when they were told to slaughter a cow. It would have been sufficient had they hastened to choose anything that could pass for a cow and slaughter it, but they asked too many questions and tried to make it hard and so God made it hard for them. They were consequently rebuked for doing so. This is why the Prophet, may God's blessings and peace be upon him, was afraid that the same thing would happen to his nation.

X

Confining Oneself to what is Lawful and Wholesome

عَنْ أَبِي هُرَيْرَةَ رَضِيَ اللَّهُ عَنْهُ قَالَ: قَالَ رَسُولُ اللَّهِ صَلَّىٰ اللَّهُ عَلَيْهِ وَسَلَّمَ: إِنَّ اللَّهَ طَيِّبٌ لَا يَقْبَلُ إِلَّا طَيِّبًا، وَإِنَّ اللَّهَ أَمَرَ الْمُؤْمِنِينَ بِمَا أَمَرَ بِهِ الْمُرْسَلِينَ فَقَالَ تَعَالَىٰ: ﴿يَا أَيُّهَا الرُّسُلُ كُلُوا مِنَ الطَّيِّبَاتِ وَاعْمَلُوا صَالِحًا﴾، وَقَالَ تَعَالَىٰ: ﴿يَا أَيُّهَا الَّذِينَ ءَامَنُوا كُلُوا مِنْ طَيِّبَاتِ مَا رَزَقْنَاكُمْ﴾ ثُمَّ ذَكَرَ الرَّجُلَ يُطِيلُ السَّفَرَ أَشْعَثَ أَغْبَرَ يَمُدُّ يَدَيْهِ إِلَىٰ السَّمَاءِ: يَا رَبِّ! يَا رَبِّ! وَمَطْعَمُهُ حَرَامٌ، وَمَشْرَبُهُ حَرَامٌ، وَمَلْبَسُهُ حَرَامٌ، وَغُذِّيَ بِالْحَرَامِ، فَأَنَّىٰ يُسْتَجَابُ لَهُ؟

رَوَاهُ مُسْلِمٌ [رقم: ١٠١٥]

On the authority of Abū Hurayrah, may God be well pleased with him, who reported that the Messenger of God, may God's blessings and peace be upon him, said: 'God Most High is exalted above any imperfection and does not accept anything save that which is wholesome. And verily, God has commanded the believers with that which He has commanded the messengers, and so He Most High said: *O Messengers, eat of the good things and do righteousness* [*al-Mu'minūn* 23: 53] and He Most High said: *O believers, eat of the good things wherewith We have provided you, and give thanks to God* [*al-Baqarah* 2: 170].' Then he mentioned a person who prolongs his travel and is dusty and dishevelled and who raises his hands to heaven, [saying]: 'O Lord! O Lord! While his food is unlawful, his drink is unlawful, his clothes are unlawful and has been nourished with the unlawful. How on earth is someone such as this likely to be answered?'

[Narrated by Muslim]

This is one of the prophetic sayings upon which are built the rules of Islam and the edifices of legal rulings. Its content encourages one to spend from one's lawful earning and prohibits spending from any other type of wealth. It also indicates that what one eats, drinks and wears must be purely lawful, free from any doubtful matter. It also teaches that whoever wants to make a request or supplication had better pay attention to this than to anything else. The saying also indicates that it is only the wholesome part of one's wealth which one spends that grows and becomes purified. Tasty food that is not permissible turns into a curse for the person who consumes it and God will not accept his works.

His saying (*Then he mentioned a person...*) means, and God knows best, this person prolongs his journeys in ways of acts of obedience, such as the pilgrimage, jihad and other acts of righteousness, yet his supplications are not answered because his food, drink and clothes are all unlawful. If this is so, how is it then for the person who is absorbed in this world or engaged in wronging others or is among those who are heedless about the different types of worship and acts of goodness?

His saying (*and he is nourished with the unlawful, how on earth is someone like this person likely to be answered?*) means: how can somebody with this characteristic be answered? This is because he does not deserve to be answered. However, it is possible that God answers his supplications out of generosity and loving kindness, and God knows best.

XI

Being Scrupulous About That Which is Doubtful

عَنْ أَبِي مُحَمَّدٍ الْحَسَنِ بْنِ عَلِيِّ بْنِ أَبِي طَالِبٍ سِبْطِ رَسُولِ اللهِ صَلَّى اللهُ عَلَيْهِ وَسَلَّمْ وَرَيْحَانَتِهِ رَضِيَ اللهُ عَنْهُمَا، قَالَ: حَفِظْتُ مِنْ رَسُولِ اللهِ صَلَّى اللهُ عَلَيْهِ وَسَلَّمْ دَعْ مَا يُرِيبُكَ إِلَى مَا لَا يُرِيبُكَ.

رَوَاهُ التِّرْمِذِيُّ [رقم: ٢٥٢٠] وَالنَّسَائِيّ [رقم: ٥٧١١]

On the authority of Abū Muhammad al-Ḥasan ibn ʿAlī ibn Abī Ṭālib – the grandson of the Messenger of God, may God's blessings and peace be upon him, and his beloved – may God be well pleased with both father and son, said: I memorized from the Messenger of God, may God's blessings and peace be upon him, 'Leave that which is doubtful for that in which there is no doubt.'

[Narrated by Tirmidhī and al-Nasā'ī.]

His saying (*that which is doubtful...*) means if you have any doubt about something, then you should leave it and go to something else in which you have no doubt. This is related to the prophetic saying VI [see p. 39] which states: 'The lawful is clearly evident and the unlawful is clearly evident and between these two are ambiguous matters....' It is also mentioned in another prophetic saying: 'A servant does not join the righteous until he leaves that which is alright for fear of falling into that which is not',[18] which is a degree higher than the one above.

XII

Leaving That Which Does Not Concern One

عَنْ أَبِي هُرَيْرَةَ رَضِيَ اللَّهُ عَنْهُ قَالَ: قَالَ رَسُولُ اللَّهِ صَلَّى اللَّهُ عَلَيْهِ وَسَلَّمَ: مِنْ حُسْنِ إِسْلَامِ الْمَرْءِ تَرْكُهُ مَا لَا يَعْنِيهِ.

رَوَاهُ التِّرْمِذِيُّ [رقم: ٢٣١٨] ابن ماجه [رقم: ٣٩٧٦]

On the authority of Abū Hurayrah, may God be well pleased with him, who reported that the Messenger of God, may God's blessings and peace be upon him, said: 'Of the signs of the perfection of a person's Islam is that he leaves that which does not concern him.'

[Narrated by Tirmidhī]

This saying was narrated by Qurrah ibn ʿAbd al-Raḥmān from al-Zuhrī from Abū Salamah from Abū Hurayrah, and he authenticated all its chains of transmission. He said about this prophetic saying: 'This is of the speech that condenses many precious meanings in a few words. A similar saying which is pregnant with many meanings despite its few words is what has been reported from Abū Dharr who said: 'Whoever considers his speech to be part of his works will speak very little except about that which concerns him.'[19]

Mālik mentioned that it has reached him that it was said to Luqmān: 'How did you get to where you are now?' They meant the merit bestowed upon him by God. He said: 'Being true in my speech, handing back trusts to their rightful owners and leaving that which does not concern me.'[20]

It is also related from al-Ḥasan that he said: 'Of the signs that God Most High has forsaken a servant is to place his preoccupation in that which does not concern him.'

Abū Dāwūd said: 'The basis of the *Sunan* in every discipline are four prophetic sayings', and he mentioned this saying among them.

XIII

The Perfection of Faith

عَنْ أَبِي حَمْزَةَ أَنَسِ بْنِ مَالِكٍ رَضِيَ اللَّهُ عَنْهُ خَادِمِ رَسُولِ اللَّهِ
صَلَّى اللَّهُ عَلَيْهِ وَسَلَّمْ عَنِ النَّبِيِّ صَلَّى اللَّهُ عَلَيْهِ وَسَلَّمْ قَالَ :
لَا يُؤْمِنُ أَحَدُكُمْ حَتَّى يُحِبَّ لِأَخِيهِ مَا يُحِبُّ لِنَفْسِهِ.

رَوَاهُ الْبُخَارِيُّ [رقم:١٣] وَمُسْلِمٌ [رقم:٤٥]

On the authority of Abū Ḥamzah Anas ibn Mālik, may God be well pleased with him – the servant of God's Messenger, may God's blessings and peace be upon him, who reported that the Prophet, may God's blessings and peace be upon him, said: 'One of you will not truly believe until he loves for his brother what he loves for himself.'

[Narrated by Bukhārī and Muslim. Thus has it been mentioned in the rigorous-ly-authenticated collection of Bukhārī 'for his brother' without any doubt. The version in the rigorously-authenticated collection of Muslim has 'his brother or neighbour', but the narrator was in doubt.]

The scholars said: it means that one shall not attain to perfect faith until one loves for his brother what one loves for oneself. Otherwise basic faith is the lot of those who do not possess this trait. What is meant is that one loves acts of obedience and permissible things for one's brother. This is evidenced by what is mentioned in the version of Nasā'ī: 'Until he loves for his brother of good what he loves for himself.' Shaykh Abū ʿAmr ibn al-Ṣalāḥ said: 'This sounds very difficult if not impossible to achieve but it is not so. This is because what this saying means is that the faith of anyone of you will not be perfect until he loves for his brother in Islam what he loves for himself. The way to do this is to like his brother to have what he likes to have for himself in a way that does not infringe on his own benefit so that the blessing that his brother enjoys is not less than the blessing that he enjoys himself. This is quite easy and within reach of the person who possesses a sound heart. It is difficult only for the corrupted heart, may God save us and all our brothers!' Abū'l-Zinād said: 'The outward meaning of this saying gives the impression of equality but its reality is preference. This is because a person likes to be better than everybody else, and if he likes for his brother what he likes for himself, it means he becomes among those who have excelled over others. Do you not see that one likes to see justice done regarding his rights and wrongs committed against him? So when he perfects his faith and his brother has with him a right that needs to be restored or an iniquity that requires setting right, he hastens to make sure that justice is done even if it is against himself or he finds it hard to do so.'

It is reported that Fuḍayl ibn ʿIyāḍ said to Sufyān ibn ʿUyaynah: 'If you want people to be like you, you have not done well by God, how about if you want them to be less than you?'

A scholar said: 'One understands from this prophetic saying that the believer with his fellow believer is like one single soul. He should therefore love for him what he loves for himself insofar as they are one single soul, as related in the other prophetic saying: "The believers are like one single body, if any limb of it suffers the rest of the body contracts fever and remains sleepless."'[21]

XIV

The Protection of Life[22]

عَنْ ابْنِ مَسْعُودٍ رَضِيَ اللّٰهُ عَنْهُ قَالَ: قَالَ رَسُولُ اللّٰهِ صَلَّى اللّٰهُ عَلَيْهِ وَسَلَّمْ: لَا يَحِلُّ دَمُ امْرِئٍ مُسْلِمٍ إِلَّا بِإِحْدَى ثَلَاثٍ: الثَّيِّبُ الزَّانِي، وَالنَّفْسُ بِالنَّفْسِ، وَالتَّارِكُ لِدِينِهِ الْمُفَارِقُ لِلْجَمَاعَةِ.

رَوَاهُ الْبُخَارِيُّ [رقم:٦٨٧٨] وَمُسْلِمٌ [رقم:١٦٧٦]

On the authority of Ibn Masʿūd, may God be well pleased with him, who reported that the Messenger of God, may God's blessings and peace be upon him, said: 'The blood of a Muslim man does not become lawful to spill except for three things: the married person who commits adultery, the person who kills another soul and the one who gives up on his religion and leaves the community.'

[Narrated by Bukhārī and Muslim]

In some of the versions that are agreed upon, it is mentioned: 'The blood of the Muslim man who bears witness that there is no god but God and that I am the Messenger of God does not become lawful to spill except for three things....' His saying (*bears witness that there is no god but God and that I am the Messenger of God*) is like an explanation of his saying (*Muslim*). Likewise, his word (*and leaves the community*) is like an explanation of (*gives up on his religion*). The blood of these three categories of people is lawful to spill by textual evidence. What is meant by community is 'the Muslims'. The person who leaves it does so by giving up on his religion which is the reason for the lawfulness of spilling his blood.

His saying (*who gives up on his religion and leaves the community*) is of general applicability to all those who commit apostasy, regardless of the kind of apostasy they commit. It is an obligation to kill such a person if he does not return to Islam.[23] The scholars stated: 'This includes anyone who abandons the community through a blameworthy innovation, transgression or something else, and God knows best.'

It seems that this is of general applicability, which includes those who assail Muslims and the like. It is permissible to kill such people to remove their harm. It could also be said about those who assail Muslims that they have left the community. It could also mean that it is not lawful to kill Muslims intentionally except in the cases of these three categories of people, and God knows best.

A scholar has concluded that the person who refrains from performing the prayer should be killed, for he is included among these three categories of people. However, there is a difference of opinion among scholars regarding this question. Some declare the person who refrains from performing the prayer to be an unbeliever while some others do not consider him to be so. Those who declare him to be an unbeliever cite as evidence the saying of the Prophet, may God's blessings and peace be upon him: 'I am commanded to fight people until they bear witness that there is no god but God and that I am the Messenger of God, establish the prayer and pay the poor-due....'[24] The reason why this saying is evidence is because he likened people's inviolability to the aggregation of the two testimonies of faith in addition to the establishment of the prayer and payment of the poor-due. Thus, anything that depends on an aggregate of things cannot occur except through the occurrence of the sum of these things and will disappear by the disappearance of the whole. This is if what is meant herein is taking that which is pronounced as evidence, which is his saying (*I am commanded to fight people...*) for this implies a command to fight for this purpose. But there seems to be here some misunderstanding for there is a difference between fighting because of something and killing for it. Fighting requires the involvement of two parties. Fighting others regarding the prayer does not imply killing for it, if one leaves the prayer without fighting others because of this abstention, and God knows best.

His saying (*the married man who commits adultery*) applies to both men and women. This is also a proof for what has been agreed upon by Muslims is that the legal ruling of committing adultery for married people is stoning but with the conditions stipulated in the books of jurisprudence.[25]

His saying (*The person who kills another soul*) confirms the words of God Most High *And therein We prescribed for them: 'A life for a life...'* [*al-Mā'idah* 5: 45]. What is meant here are souls that are equal in the profession of Islam and freedom from bondage. The proof for this is the saying of the Prophet, may God's blessings and peace be upon him, 'A Muslim is not killed for killing an unbeliever.'[26] Likewise, freedom from bondage is a condition of equality according to Mālik, Shāfiʿī and Aḥmad. The proponents of personal views were of the opinion that a Muslim must be killed if he kills a *dhimmī* and the free person must be killed for killing a slave, and they may use this saying as a proof for their opinion. However, the majority of scholars have a different view.[27]

XV

Islamic Manners

عَنْ أَبِي هُرَيْرَةَ رَضِيَ اللَّهُ عَنْهُ أَنَّ رَسُولَ اللَّهِ صَلَّى اللَّهُ عَلَيْهِ
وَسَلَّمْ قَالَ: مَنْ كَانَ يُؤْمِنُ بِاللَّهِ وَالْيَوْمِ الْآخِرِ فَلْيَقُلْ خَيْرًا
أَوْ لِيَصْمُتْ، وَمَنْ كَانَ يُؤْمِنُ بِاللَّهِ وَالْيَوْمِ الْآخِرِ فَلْيُكْرِمْ جَارَهُ،
وَمَنْ كَانَ يُؤْمِنُ بِاللَّهِ وَالْيَوْمِ الْآخِرِ فَلْيُكْرِمْ ضَيْفَهُ.

رَوَاهُ الْبُخَارِيُّ [رقم:٦٠١٨] وَمُسْلِمٌ [رقم:٤٧]

On the authority of Abū Hurayrah, may God be well pleased with him, who reported that the Messenger of God, may God's blessings and peace be upon him, said: 'Whoever believes in God and the Last Day let him say something good or else keep quiet. And whoever believes in God and the Last Day let him honour his neighbour. And whoever believes in God and the Last Day let him honour his guest.'

[Narrated by Bukhārī and Muslim]

His saying (*whoever believes in God and the Last Day*) means whoever believes fully, with a complete faith that saves from God's chastisement and leads to God's good pleasure, let him (*say something good or else keep quiet*). This is because the person who truly believes in God fears His threats, hopes for His reward and strives to do what He commands and refrains from what He prohibits. The most important thing in this process is to control his limbs which are his subjects and, therefore, he is responsible for them, as God Most High said, *the hearing, the sight, the heart – all of those shall be questioned of* [*al-Isrā'* 17: 36], *not a word he utters, but by him is an observer ready* [*Qāf* 50: 18].

The defects of the tongue are numerous. This is why the Prophet, may God's blessings and peace be upon him, said: 'Are people thrown in the Fire on their nostrils except for that which their tongues have reaped?'[28] He also said, may God's blessings and peace be upon him: 'All the speech of the son of Adam will be against him except for the remembrance of God Most High, enjoining the good and forbidding the wrong.'[29] Whoever knows this and truly believes in it will fear God with regard to his tongue and will only utter that which is good or else keep silent.

One scholar mentioned that all the proprieties of goodness are derived from four prophetic sayings and he mentioned among them the saying of the Prophet, may God's blessings and peace be upon him: 'Whoever believes in God and the Last Day let him say something good or else keep silent.'

Another scholar said: 'When a person wants to speak, he should first think: if what he is going to say is definitely good and he is going to be rewarded for it, then he should speak. Otherwise he should refrain from speaking whether what he is going to say appears to be unlawful, offensive or permissible. Hence, he is commanded to refrain from permissible speech, for it is recommended to do so, out of fear that it may lead him to speech that is forbidden or offensive, and this may happen quite frequently. God Most High said: *not a word he utters, but by him is an observer ready* [*Qāf* 50: 18].

The scholars have different views about whether everything uttered by a person is recorded, even if it happens to be permissible, or whether only that in which there is re-ward or punishment is recorded. The latter view is the view of Ibn ʿAbbās and some other eminent scholars. The noble verse [*Qāf* 50: 18] is therefore of particular applicability to the speech that involves a requital.

His saying (*let him honour his neighbour... let him honour his guest*) points to the rights of the neighbour and guest and the necessity of being kind to them and of protecting one's limbs. In His Book, God Most High has enjoined being kind towards neighbours. The Prophet, may God's blessings and peace be upon him, said: 'Gabriel, peace be upon him, kept on enjoining me to take care of the neighbour until I feared he was going to make him among one's inheritors.'[30]

Giving hospitality is part of Islam as well as being the characteristic of the prophets and righteous people. Some scholars declared it to be an obligation, but most scholars are of the opinion that it is of the noble character traits. The author of *al-Ifṣāḥ* wrote: 'Among the things that one understands from this prophetic saying is that honouring the guest is an act of worship, which is neither diminished by hosting a rich person nor is it changed by giving one's guest whatever little one has. To honour a guest consists of showing him a happy mien and engaging him in good conversation. But the heart of offering hospitality lies in providing food. One has to hasten therefore to provide whatever God has made available without any display of affectation.' The same scholar went on to mention a few things about offering hospitality until he said: 'As for his saying (*let him say something good or else keep quiet*), this indicates that the utterance of that which is good is better than keeping quiet, while silence is better than saying something bad. Included in the utterance of what is good is to convey from God and from His Messenger, may God's blessings and peace be upon him, teaching the Muslims, enjoining the good with full knowledge of what one is doing and forbidding the wrong also with full knowledge, reconciling between people and saying fair things to them. The best speech is to utter a word of truth in front of someone who is feared or sought in matters of substantiation [of claims] and settlement [of disputes].'

XVI

Warning Against Anger

عَنْ أَبِي هُرَيْرَةَ رَضِيَ اللهُ عَنْهُ أَنَّ رَجُلًا قَالَ لِلنَّبِيِّ صَلَّى اللهُ عَلَيْهِ وَسَلَّمْ: أَوْصِنِي. قَالَ: لَا تَغْضَبْ، فَرَدَّدَ مِرَارًا، قَالَ: لَا تَغْضَبْ.

رَوَاهُ الْبُخَارِيُّ [رقم:٦١١٦]

On the authority of Abū Hurayrah, may God be well pleased with him, who reported that a man said to the Prophet, may God's blessings and peace be upon him: 'Advise me!' He said: 'Do not get angry!', and he repeated it several times, saying, 'Do not get angry!'

[Narrated by Bukhārī]

The author of *al-Ifṣāḥ* wrote: 'It is possible that the Prophet, may God's blessings and peace be upon him, knew that this man was often prone to anger and so he singled him out with this advice. The Prophet, may God's blessings and peace be upon him, praised the person who controls himself when angry, saying: 'The hard person is not the one who overcomes others through his physical strength but rather the one who controls himself when he gets angry.'[31] God Most High also praised such a person in His saying, *and restrain their rage, and pardon the offences of their fellowmen* [*Āl ʿImrān* 3: 134]. It is reported that the Prophet, may God's blessings and peace be upon him, said: 'Whoever controls his anger when he is in a position to vent it, God will call him in front of all created beings on the Day of Judgement and let him choose the houris he would like to have.'[32] It is also related in a prophetic saying: 'Anger is from the Devil';[33] this is why it affects a person's balance and makes him utter falsehood, commit that which is censured, and harbour rancour and hatred, as well as other forbidden, shameful deeds. All this is the result of anger. We seek refuge in God from it! It is reported in the prophetic saying related by Sulaymān ibn Surd that: 'Seeking refuge in God from the accursed Devil takes anger away.'[34] This is because it is the Devil who embellishes anger and everything that has catastrophic results. The Devil entices the angry person and takes him far from God's good pleasure, so seeking refuge in God from him is one of the most effective weapons to drive away the Devil's stratagem.

XVII

Allah Has Ordained Kindness in every Matter[35]

عَنْ أَبِي يَعْلَى شَدَّادِ بْنِ أَوْسٍ رَضِيَ اللَّهُ عَنْهُ عَنْ رَسُولِ اللَّهِ صَلَّى اللَّهُ عَلَيْهِ وَسَلَّمَ قَالَ: إِنَّ اللَّهَ كَتَبَ الْإِحْسَانَ عَلَى كُلِّ شَيْءٍ، فَإِذَا قَتَلْتُمْ فَأَحْسِنُوا الْقِتْلَةَ، وَإِذَا ذَبَحْتُمْ فَأَحْسِنُوا الذِّبْحَةَ، وَلْيُحِدَّ أَحَدُكُمْ شَفْرَتَهُ، وَلْيُرِحْ ذَبِيحَتَهُ.

رَوَاهُ مُسْلِمٌ [رقم: ١٩٥٥]

On the authority of Abū Yaʿlā Shaddād ibn Aws, may God be well pleased with him, who reported that the Messenger of God, may God's blessings and peace be upon him, said: 'God has decreed kindness in everything. So when you kill, kill well, and when you sacrifice an animal, do it well. Let one of you sharpen his knife and spare his sacrificial animal any suffering.'

[Narrated by Muslim]

His saying (*kill well*) is of general applicability in cases of killing, whether it is a question of slaughtering animals, killing in retaliation, applying a fixed punishment or something similar. This prophetic saying combines a multitude of rules. What is meant by 'exercising restraint' is that one strives to do the job effectively and not aim to inflict torture. With regard to beasts, it is that one be gentle with them such that one does not kill them with a sudden move of his knife, nor drag them from one place to another; one should direct them towards the direction of the *qiblah*, pronounce the *basmalah*, apply the knife forcefully, cut the throat and jugular veins and leave them until they become cold. One should acknowledge God's favour and thank Him for His blessings. For He has made subservient to us that which He could easily have set against us, and made lawful for us that which, if He willed, He would have made unlawful.

XVIII

Good Character

عَـنْ أَبِي ذَرٍّ جُنْدُبِ بْنِ جُنَادَةَ، وَأَبِي عَبْدِ الرَّحْمَنِ مُعَاذِ بْنِ جَبَلٍ رَضِيَ اللهُ عَنْهُمَا، عَـنْ رَسُولِ اللهِ صَلَّى اللهُ عَلَيْهِ وَسَلَّمَ قَـالَ: اتَّقِ اللهَ حَيْثُمَا كُنْتَ، وَأَتْبِعِ السَّيِّئَةَ الْحَسَنَةَ تَمْحُهَا، وَخَالِقِ النَّاسَ بِخُلُقٍ حَسَنٍ.

رَوَاهُ التِّرْمِذِيُّ [رقم:١٩٨٧]

On the authority of Abū Dharr Jundub ibn Junāda and Abū ʿAbd al-Raḥmān Muʿādh ibn Jabal, may God be well pleased with both of them, who reported that the Messenger of God, may God's blessings and peace be upon him, said: 'Fear God wherever you may be, follow a bad deed with a good one and you will erase it, and behave graciously with people.'

[Narrated by Tirmidhī]

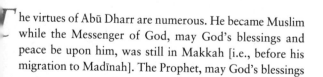

The virtues of Abū Dharr are numerous. He became Muslim while the Messenger of God, may God's blessings and peace be upon him, was still in Makkah [i.e., before his migration to Madīnah]. The Prophet, may God's blessings and peace be upon him, commanded him to join his own people. However, when he saw his keenness to stay with him in Makkah and knew that was not possible for him, he said to him, God's blessings and peace be upon him: 'Fear God wherever you may be, and follow a bad deed with a good one and you will erase it.' This conforms to God's words in the Qur'ān: *surely the good deeds will drive away the evil deeds* [*Hūd* 11: 114].

His saying (*and behave graciously with people*) means: treat people as you wish they would treat you and know that, 'The heaviest thing that is put on the Scale [on the Day of Judgement] is good character.'[36] The Messenger of God, God's blessings and peace be upon him, said: 'The most beloved of you to me, who are sat closest to me on the Day of Judgement, are those of you who have the best character.'[37]

Good character is from the traits of the prophets and messengers. The best among the believers do not reward a bad deed with a similar one. Rather, they forgive and excuse others and show kindness even to those who harm them.

XIX

Watch Out for God, He Will Watch Out for You

عَنْ عَبْدِ اللَّهِ بْنِ عَبَّاسٍ رَضِيَ اللَّهُ عَنْهُمَا قَالَ: كُنْتُ خَلْفَ رَسُولِ اللَّهِ صَلَّى اللَّهُ عَلَيْهِ وَسَلَّمْ يَوْمًا، فَقَالَ: يَا غُلَامُ! إِنِّي أُعَلِّمُكَ كَلِمَاتٍ: احْفَظِ اللَّهَ يَحْفَظْكَ، احْفَظِ اللَّهَ تَجِدْهُ تُجَاهَكَ، إِذَا سَأَلْتَ فَاسْأَلِ اللَّهَ، وَإِذَا اسْتَعَنْتَ فَاسْتَعِنْ بِاللَّهِ، وَاعْلَمْ أَنَّ الْأُمَّةَ لَوْ اجْتَمَعَتْ عَلَى أَنْ يَنْفَعُوكَ بِشَيْءٍ لَمْ يَنْفَعُوكَ إِلَّا بِشَيْءٍ قَدْ كَتَبَهُ اللَّهُ لَكَ، وَإِنِ اجْتَمَعُوا عَلَى أَنْ يَضُرُّوكَ بِشَيْءٍ لَمْ يَضُرُّوكَ إِلَّا بِشَيْءٍ قَدْ كَتَبَهُ اللَّهُ عَلَيْكَ، رُفِعَتِ الْأَقْلَامُ، وَجَفَّتِ الصُّحُفُ.

رَوَاهُ التِّرْمِذِيُّ [رقم: ٢٥١٦]

وَفِي رِوَايَةِ غَيْرِ التِّرْمِذِيِّ: احْفَظِ اللَّهَ تَجِدْهُ أَمَامَكَ، تَعَرَّفْ إِلَى اللَّهِ فِي الرَّخَاءِ يَعْرِفْكَ فِي الشِّدَّةِ، وَاعْلَمْ أَنَّ مَا أَخْطَأَكَ لَمْ يَكُنْ لِيُصِيبَكَ، وَمَا أَصَابَكَ لَمْ يَكُنْ لِيُخْطِئَكَ، وَاعْلَمْ أَنَّ النَّصْرَ مَعَ الصَّبْرِ، وَأَنَّ الْفَرَجَ مَعَ الْكَرْبِ، وَأَنَّ مَعَ الْعُسْرِ يُسْرًا.

On the authority of Abū'l-ʿAbbās ʿAbd Allāh ibn ʿAbbās, may God be well pleased with them, who said: I was one day behind the Prophet, God's blessings and peace be upon him, when he said: 'O lad! I will teach you a few things: watch out for God and God will watch out for you. Watch out for God and you will find Him before you. When you make a request, make it to God, and when you seek help, seek it from God. And know that if the whole nation were to gather to benefit you with something, they would not benefit you except with something that God has decreed for you. And if the whole nation were to gather to harm you with something, they would not harm you except with something that God has decreed for you. The pens have been lifted and the scrolls have dried.'

[Narrated by Tirmidhī. In the version by other than Tirmidhī, it is reported: 'Watch out for God, and you will find Him in front of you. Know God in times of ease, and He will know you in times of hardship. And know that that which has missed you could not have befallen you, and that which has befallen you could not have missed you. And know that triumph comes with forbearance and with hardship comes ease.']

The virtues of our master Ibn ʿAbbās are also too many to enumerate. The Prophet, God's blessings and peace be upon him, prayed for him, saying: 'O God! Grant him understanding of the religion and teach him interpretation [of the Qur'ān].'[38] He also prayed that he be granted wisdom twice.[39] It is also confirmed from him that he saw Gabriel twice.[40] He is the scholar par excellence of the Muslim nation and its sea of knowledge. The Messenger of God, God's blessings and peace be upon him, saw him fit for advice despite his tender age and told him to (*Watch out for God*), which means to be obedient to your Lord, carrying out His commands and avoiding His prohibitions.

His saying (*Watch out for God and you will find Him before you*) means: work for Him by obeying Him and do not let Him see you contravening Him, and, if you do so, you will find Him before you upon the advent of hardships. An illustration of this is the story of the three men who took shelter in a cave to protect themselves from the rain. The entrance of the cave was later blocked by a huge rock. They enjoined one other to seek God through the righteous works they had done in the hope that God would save them. Each one of them mentioned an incident that happened to him with his Lord, and, as each of them did so, the rock moved slightly to one side and they were able to get out of the cave. The story of these three men is well known in the rigorously-authenticated collections of prophetic sayings.[41]

His saying (*when you make a request, make it to God and when you seek help, seek it from God*) teaches him to rely on his Master such that he takes as Deity none save Him and such that he does not attach himself to anyone except Him regarding all matters, whether they are great or small. God Most High says: *And whosoever fears God, He will appoint for him a way out* [*al-Ṭalāq* 65: 3]. Insofar as a person inclines towards other than God Most High in his requests, with his heart or hope, he has turned away from his Lord in favour of him who neither benefits nor harms him. And the same applies to being fearful of other than God. The Prophet, God's blessings and peace be upon him, emphasized this by saying (*And know that if the whole nation were to gather to benefit you with something, they would not benefit you except with something that God has decreed for you*). And the same applies to harm. This is faith in the Decree, which is obligatory, whether it be good or bad. If the believer is certain of this, then what is the benefit of making a request to other than God or seeking help from other than Him? This is also illustrated by the reply of the Patriarch Ibrahim, peace be upon him, to Gabriel, peace be upon him, when he asked him in mid-air: 'Do you need anything?' 'From you? No,' the Prophet Ibrāhīm, peace be upon him, replied.[42]

His saying (*The pens are lifted and the scrolls have dried*) is a confirmation of what has been mentioned above, i.e., it will not be different than what I have mentioned either through abrogation or alteration.

He then said (*And know that triumph comes with forbearance and that relief comes with suffering and ease comes after hardship*), and so he drew attention to the fact that, in this world, people, and especially the righteous among them, are exposed to calamities due to God's words, exalted is He, *Surely We will try you with something of fear and hunger, and diminution of goods and lives and fruits; yet give thou good tidings unto the patient who, when they are visited by an affliction, say, 'Surely we belong to God, and to Him we return'; upon those rest blessings and mercy from their Lord, and those – they are the truly guided* [*al-Baqarah* 2: 155–158] and His saying, *Surely the patient will be paid their wages in full without reckoning* [*al-Zumar* 39: 10].

XX

Shame Is Part of Faith

عَنْ أَبِي مَسْعُودٍ عُقْبَةَ بْنِ عَمْرٍو الْأَنْصَارِيِّ الْبَدْرِيِّ رَضِيَ اللهُ
عَنْهُ قَالَ: قَالَ رَسُولُ اللهِ صَلَّى اللهُ عَلَيْهِ وَسَلَّمْ: إِنَّ مِمَّا أَدْرَكَ
النَّاسُ مِنْ كَلَامِ النُّبُوَّةِ الْأُولَى: إِذَا لَمْ تَسْتَحِ فَاصْنَعْ مَا شِئْتَ.
رَوَاهُ الْبُخَارِيُّ [رقم: ٣٤٨٣]

On the authority of Abū Masʿūd ʿUqbah ibn ʿAmr al-Anṣārī al-Badrī, may God be well pleased with him, who reported that the Messenger of God, God's blessings and peace be upon him, said: 'Of that which has reached people of the speech of earlier prophecy, "If you have no shame, do as you wish."'

[Narrated by Bukhārī]

The meaning of (*of the speech of earlier prophecy*) is that shame has always been praiseworthy, appreciated and commanded, and that it has not been abrogated by the revealed laws of earlier prophets.

His saying (*do as you wish*) can be understood in two ways. The first is that it is a form of threat rather than a command to engage in whatever one wishes. This is like the words of God, *Those who blaspheme Our signs are not hidden from Us. What, is he who shall be cast into the Fire better, or he who comes on the Day of Resurrection in security? Do what you will; surely He sees the things you do* [*Fuṣṣilat* 41: 40–43], which are a threat, for God has shown them what they should do and what they should avoid. It is also like the saying of the Prophet, God's blessings and peace be upon him: 'Whoever sells wine, let him slaughter and cut pigs for his consumption',[43] which does not mean that pigs are lawful to slaughter and consume. The second way to understand these words is: go ahead and engage in everything that people feel ashamed to engage in, i.e., when the perpetuator of a shameful deed is openly known. An example of this is the saying of the Prophet, God's blessings and peace be upon him: 'Shame is part of faith',[44] which means because it stops the person who has it from engaging in indecent acts and prompts him to engage in virtuous and good deeds, just as faith does. Shame has become like faith because they both achieve the same result, and God knows best.

XXI

Say 'I believe in God' and then Be Upright

عَنْ أَبِي عَمْرٍو - وَقِيلَ أَبِي عَمْرَةَ - سُفْيَانَ بْنِ عَبْدِ اللهِ رَضِيَ اللهُ عَنْهُ قَالَ: قُلْتُ: يَا رَسُولَ اللهِ! قُلْ لِي فِي الْإِسْلَامِ قَوْلًا لَا أَسْأَلُ عَنْهُ أَحَدًا غَيْرَكَ. قَالَ: قُلْ آمَنْتُ بِاللهِ ثُمَّ اسْتَقِمْ.

رَوَاهُ مُسْلِمٌ [رقم:٣٨]

On the authority of Abū ʿAmr – Abū ʿAmrah in some narrations – Sufyān ibn ʿAbd Allāh al-Thaqafī, may God be well pleased with him, who said: I said, 'O Messenger of God! Tell me something relating to Islam about which I will not ask anyone else after you.' He said: 'Say I believe in God, and then be upright.'

[Narrated by Muslim]

The meaning of (*Tell me something relating to Islam about which I will not ask anyone else after you*) is: teach me something comprehensive that encompasses the meaning of Islam such that it does not require the explanation of anyone else so that I can act upon it and fear God through it. The Prophet, God's blessings and peace be upon him, responded by saying (*Say 'I believe in God' and then be upright*).

This is of the most comprehensive, concise speech granted to the Prophet, God's blessings and peace be upon him, for he has gathered, for the questioner, in these few words all the meanings of submission (*islām*) and faith (*īmān*). He commanded him to renew his faith using his tongue while remembering with his heart. He also commanded him to be upright in pursuing the works of obedience and refraining from all contraventions. This is because being upright will not happen if there is the slightest crookedness, for crookedness works against it. This is reminiscent of the words of God Most High, *Those who have said, 'Our Lord is God', then have gone straight* [*Fuṣṣilat* 41: 30], i.e., believed in God alone and then were upright and steadfast in their belief and obedience until God took their souls away in this state. ʿUmar ibn al-Khaṭṭāb said, may God be well pleased with him, said: 'By God, they were upright and steadfast in His obedience and did not use sly tricks like foxes do.' It means that they were assidu- ous in performing most acts of obedience, whether in relation to belief, speech or action, and persisted in performing them. This is the meaning chosen by most Qur'ān exegetes, and it is also the meaning of the above prophetic saying, God willing. Likewise, His words, glory be to Him, *So go you straight, as you have been commanded* [*Hūd* 11: 112] about which Ibn ʿAbbās said: 'Of all the Qurānic verses revealed to the Messenger of God, God's blessings and peace be upon him, none was harder on him than this verse. This is why he said: "*Hūd* and its sister-*sūrah*s have turned my hair grey."'[45]

Abū'l-Qāsim al-Qushayrī, may God have mercy on him, said: 'Being upright is a degree through which perfected and completed matters are achieved; with its existence, good things and their arrangement take place. Whoever is not straight in his striving, his striving is lost and his effort comes to nothing. No one can withstand being upright except the most perfected of men, for it entails leaving habitual matters and things, shunning formalities and customs and standing before God Most High with genuine sincerity. This is why the Prophet, God's blessings and peace be upon him, said: "Be upright and you shall not be able to do so...."'[46] Al-Wāsiṭī said: 'Being upright is the character trait through which all good qualities are perfected. With its loss, all good qualities become ugly,' and God knows best.

XXII

Confining Oneself to what is Obligated Will Take One to Paradise

عَنْ أَبِي عَبْدِ اللهِ جَابِرِ بْنِ عَبْدِ اللهِ الأَنْصَارِيِّ رَضِيَ اللهُ عَنْهُمَا: أَنَّ رَجُلًا سَأَلَ رَسُولَ اللهِ صَلَّى اللهُ عَلَيْهِ وَسَلَّمْ فَقَالَ: أَرَأَيْتَ إِذَا صَلَّيْتُ الْمَكْتُوبَاتِ، وَصُمْتُ رَمَضَانَ، وَأَحْلَلْتُ الْحَلَالَ، وَحَرَّمْتُ الْحَرَامَ، وَلَمْ أَزِدْ عَلَى ذَلِكَ شَيْئًا أَأَدْخُلُ الْجَنَّةَ؟ قَالَ: نَعَمْ.

رَوَاهُ مُسْلِمٌ [رقم:١٥]

On the authority of Abū ʿAbd Allāh Jābir ibn ʿAbd Allāh al-Anṣārī, may God be well pleased with both, who reported that a man asked the Messenger of God, God's blessings and peace be upon him, saying: 'Would I enter Paradise if I confine myself to praying the five prescribed prayers, fasting the month of Ramadan, declare what is lawful to be lawful and what is unlawful to be unlawful, and do not add anything else to these?' He said: 'Yes, indeed!'

[Narrated by Muslim]

The man who asked this question was al-Nuʿmān ibn Qawqal. Shaykh ʿAmr ibn al-Ṣalāḥ said: 'It seems that what he meant by his saying "declared that which is unlawful to be unlawful" are two things: the first is that he believes them to be unlawful, and the second is that he does not engage in them, in contrast to declaring something to be lawful, for he needs only to believe it to be lawful and does not need necessarily to engage in it.'

The author of the *Mufhim* wrote: 'The Prophet, God's blessings and peace be upon him, did not mention to the questioner anything about voluntary works on the whole, which indicates that it is permissible to leave voluntary works on the whole. However, whoever leaves them and does not perform at least some of them would miss a tremendous benefit and momentous reward. And whoever leaves continually some of the Sunnahs, this will constitute a defect in his religion and a flaw in his credibility. If he leaves them out of neglect and distaste, then this is considered a form of corruption for which he deserves to be censured. Our scholars have said: 'If the inhabitants of a township were to conspire to leave a prophetic practice, they have to be struggled against until they go back on their decision.' The Companions, may God be well pleased with them, and those who came after them, were as diligent in practising the prophetic practices and other virtuous works as they were in performing the obligations. They did not make any distinction between the former and the latter as far as seizing the opportunity of gaining reward was concerned.

The leading Muslim jurists needed to mention the difference between the obligatory duties and non-obligatory ones because of what this implies of the necessity of repeating them or not repeating them, out of fear of punishment for leaving them, or its negation if leaving them happens in a certain way.

The Prophet, God's blessings and peace be upon him, did not draw the man's attention to other prophetic practices because he was new to Islam. He did not want to repel him by mentioning too many things. The Prophet, God's blessings and peace be upon him, knew that once this man became firm in his Islam and God expanded his breast, he would desire what other Muslims desire. Or it could be that the Prophet, God's blessings and peace be upon him, did not want this man to think that other prophetic practices and voluntary works were obligatory and so he left it at that.

Also in the other prophetic saying it is reported that a man asked the Prophet, God's blessings and peace be upon him, about the prayer and he informed him that they were five prayers in total. The man asked: 'Do I have to do more prayers?' He said: 'No, unless you want to offer voluntary prayers.' Then he asked him about fasting, the pilgrimage and other legal prescriptions, and the Prophet, God's blessings and peace be upon him, answered him and the man said at the end: 'By God, I will not add to this or take away anything.' Upon which the Prophet, God's blessings and peace be upon him, said: 'He is successful if he keeps to his word, ' and in another narration, 'He will enter Paradise if he holds fast to what he has been commanded.'[47]

The prophetic practices and voluntary works have been prescribed to perfect the obligatory works. This questioner and the one before him were left alone by the Prophet, God's blessings and peace be upon him, in order to make it easy on them until such time that their hearts were opened by understanding from him and the desire to perform supererogatory acts arose in them. When this happens, performing those acts becomes easy.

Such a person increases through his perseverance in performing the obligations in their due time without any fault, thus gaining success, a great deal of success. And whoever performs the obligations and follows them with supererogatory acts will gain more success than him.

XXIII

Hastening to Do Good

عَنْ ابْنِ مَالِكٍ - الحَارِثِ بْنِ الحَارِثِ - الْأَشْعَرِيِّ رَضِيَ اللّٰهُ عَنْهُ قَالَ: قَالَ رَسُولُ اللّٰهِ صَلَّىٰ اللّٰهُ عَلَيْهِ وَسَلَّمْ: الطُّهُورُ شَطْرُ الْإِيمَانِ، وَالْحَمْدُ لِلّٰهِ تَمْلَأُ الْمِيزَانَ، وَسُبْحَانَ اللّٰهِ وَالْحَمْدُ لِلّٰهِ تَمْلَآنِ - أَوْ تَمْلَأُ - مَا بَيْنَ السَّمَاءِ وَالْأَرْضِ، وَالصَّلَاةُ نُورٌ، وَالصَّدَقَةُ بُرْهَانٌ، وَالصَّبْرُ ضِيَاءٌ، وَالْقُرْآنُ حُجَّةٌ لَكَ أَوْ عَلَيْكَ، كُلُّ النَّاسِ يَغْدُو فَبَايِعٌ نَفْسَهُ فَمُعْتِقُهَا أَوْ مُوبِقُهَا.

رَوَاهُ مُسْلِمٌ [رقم: ٢٢٣]

On the authority of Ibn Mālik – al-Hārith ibn al-Ḥārith – al-Ashʿarī, may God be well pleased with him, who reported that the Messenger of God, God's blessings and peace be upon him, said: 'The act of purity is half of faith and "praise be to God" fills the Scale, and "glory be to God and praise be to God". fill what is between heaven and earth. And the prayer is light, charity is proof, [and] patience is brightness, while the Qur'ān is proof for or against you. All people strive for their own souls: there are some who sell their souls and free them, while others lead them to destruction.'

[Narrated by Muslim]

This prophetic saying is one of the foundations of Islam and contains very important rules of the religion as a whole. There is a difference of opinion concerning the meaning of (*The act of purity is half of faith*). Some are of the opinion that the reward for the act of purity could reach to half of that of faith. It is also said that what is meant by faith here is the prayer. God Most High says in the Qur'ān, *but God would never leave your faith to waste* [*al-Baqarah* 2: 143]. Purity is a condition for the validity of the prayer, and so it has become like its half, even though it does not have to be a real half.

As for his saying (*and 'praise be to God' fills the Scale*), it means that due to the tremendousness of its reward, it fills the scale of the person praising God Most High. The texts of the Qur'ān and the Prophetic Practice concur about the weight of works and the heaviness and lightness of people's works on the Day of Judgement.

Likewise, his saying (*and 'glory be to God' and 'praise be to God' fill what is between heaven and earth*) means that their reward is tremendous. The reason for the tremendousness of their merit is due to what they contain of the meanings of God's transcendence and people's indigence with regard to Him.

And his saying, God's blessings and peace be upon him, (*and the prayer is light*) means that it prevents from disobedience, warns against indecency, and guides to that which is right, just as light is used to see what is around one. It is also said that its meaning is that its end will be a light for the person who performs it on the Day of Judgement. And it is also said that it means it will be a manifest light on the face of the praying person on the Day of Judgement, while in this world splendour appears on his face in contrast to the person who does not pray, and God knows best.

As for his saying, God's blessings and peace be upon him, (*and charity is proof*), the author of *al-Tajrīd* wrote: 'It means that one takes refuge in it in the same way one resorts to proofs. It is as if when the servant shall be asked on the Day of Judgement how he spent his wealth, his acts of charity will be proofs for his answer to such a question. This servant will say: "I spent it in charity."' Another scholar said: 'The act of charity is proof for the faith of its doer, for the hypocrite refrains from doing it due to his lack of faith in it. Hence, whoever gives to charity, one can infer from his charity that he has a strong faith,' and God knows best.

As for his saying, God's blessings and peace be upon him, (*and patience is brightness*), this refers to patience that is praiseworthy according to the Sacred Law, which means being patient in the obedience of God Most High, and being patient in refraining from disobeying Him. It also refers to patience upon the advent of misfortunes and different types of adversities in this world. What is meant is that patience is praiseworthy and one uses it as one would use light in the dark to guide one to one's destination and to keep one on the right path. Ibrāhīm al-Khawwāṣ said: 'Patience is tantamount to being firm in following the Qur'ān and the Prophetic Practice.' It is also said: 'Patience is facing tribulation with good manners.' Abū ʿAlī al-Daqqāq said, may God have mercy on him, 'Patience is not to object to what has been destined. As for manifesting tribulation in the form of complaint, this does not negate patience.' Regarding Ayyūb, peace be upon him, God Most High said, *Surely We found him a steadfast man. How excellent a servant he was! He was a penitent* [*Ṣād* 38: 44] even though He said, *Behold, affliction has visited me, and You are the most merciful of the merciful* [*al-Anbiyā'* 21: 83], and God knows best.

As for his saying, God's blessings and peace be upon him, (*And the Qur'ān is a proof for or against you*), its meaning is very clear: if you recite and act on it, you will benefit. Otherwise it is a proof against you.

His saying (*All people strive for their own souls: there are those who sell their souls and free them, while others lead them to destruction*) means that every human being endeavours to do something for his own soul. Some sell their souls to God through His obedience and thus deliver them from God's chastisement, as God Most High says, *God has bought from the believers their selves and their possessions against the gift of Paradise* [*al-Tawbah* 9: 111]. Others sell their souls to the Devil and folly by following their whims and thereby cause their own ruin. O God, grant us success to work in Your obedience and to avoid destroying ourselves through disobeying You.

XXIV

The Prohibition of Oppression

عَنْ أَبِي ذَرٍّ الْغِفَارِيِّ رَضِيَ اللَّهُ عَنْهُ عَنْ النَّبِيِّ صَلَّى اللَّهُ عَلَيْهِ وَسَلَّمْ فِيمَا يَرْوِيهِ عَنْ رَبِّهِ تَبَارَكَ وَتَعَالَىٰ، أَنَّهُ قَالَ: يَا عِبَادِي: إِنِّي حَرَّمْتُ الظُّلْمَ عَلَىٰ نَفْسِي، وَجَعَلْتُهُ بَيْنَكُمْ مُحَرَّمًا فَلَا تَظَالَمُوا. يَا عِبَادِي! كُلُّكُمْ ضَالٌّ إِلَّا مَنْ هَدَيْتُهُ، فَاسْتَهْدُونِي أَهْدِكُمْ. يَا عِبَادِي! كُلُّكُمْ جَائِعٌ إِلَّا مَنْ أَطْعَمْتُهُ، فَاسْتَطْعِمُونِي أُطْعِمْكُمْ. يَا عِبَادِي! كُلُّكُمْ عَارٍ إِلَّا مَنْ كَسَوْتُهُ، فَاسْتَكْسُونِي أَكْسُكُمْ. يَا عِبَادِي! إِنَّكُمْ تُخْطِئُونَ بِاللَّيْلِ وَالنَّهَارِ، وَأَنَا أَغْفِرُ الذُّنُوبَ جَمِيعًا فَاسْتَغْفِرُونِي أَغْفِرْ لَكُمْ. يَا عِبَادِي! إِنَّكُمْ لَنْ تَبْلُغُوا ضَرِّي فَتَضُرُّونِي، وَلَنْ تَبْلُغُوا نَفْعِي فَتَنْفَعُونِي. يَا عِبَادِي! لَوْ أَنَّ أَوَّلَكُمْ وَآخِرَكُمْ وَإِنْسَكُمْ وَجِنَّكُمْ كَانُوا عَلَىٰ أَتْقَىٰ قَلْبِ رَجُلٍ وَاحِدٍ مِنْكُمْ، مَا زَادَ ذَلِكَ فِي مُلْكِي شَيْئًا. يَا عِبَادِي!

لَوْ أَنَّ أَوَّلَكُمْ وَآخِرَكُمْ وَإِنْسَكُمْ وَجِنَّكُمْ كَانُوا عَلَىٰ أَفْجَرِ قَلْبِ رَجُلٍ وَاحِدٍ مِنْكُمْ، مَا نَقَصَ ذَلِكَ مِنْ مُلْكِي شَيْئًا. يَا عِبَادِي! لَوْ أَنَّ أَوَّلَكُمْ وَآخِرَكُمْ وَإِنْسَكُمْ وَجِنَّكُمْ قَامُوا فِي صَعِيدٍ وَاحِدٍ، فَسَأَلُونِي، فَأَعْطَيْتُ كُلَّ وَاحِدٍ مَسْأَلَتَهُ، مَا نَقَصَ ذَلِكَ مِمَّا عِنْدِي إِلَّا كَمَا يَنْقُصُ الْمِخْيَطُ إِذَا أُدْخِلَ الْبَحْرَ. يَا عِبَادِي! إِنَّمَا هِيَ أَعْمَالُكُمْ أُحْصِيهَا لَكُمْ، ثُمَّ أُوَفِّيكُمْ إِيَّاهَا. فَمَنْ وَجَدَ خَيْرًا فَلْيَحْمَدِ اللَّهَ، وَمَنْ وَجَدَ غَيْرَ ذَلِكَ فَلَا يَلُومَنَّ إِلَّا نَفْسَهُ.

رَوَاهُ مُسْلِمٌ [رقم: ٢٥٧٧]

On the authority of Abū Dharr al-Ghifārī, may God be well pleased with him, who related that the Messenger of God, God's blessings and peace be upon him, reported his Lord, glorified and exalted is He, as saying: 'O My servants! I have prohibited oppression for Myself and made it prohibited amongst you, so do not oppress one another. O My servants! You are all misguided except him whom I guide, so seek guidance from Me, for I will guide you. O My servants! You are all hungry except him whom I feed, so ask for food from Me, and I will feed you. O My servants! You are all nude except him whom I clothe, so ask Me for raiment, and I will dress you. O My servants! You err night and day and I forgive all sins, so seek My forgiveness, and I will forgive you. O My servants! You will never attain to a position such that you can harm Me, nor will you ever attain to a position such that you can benefit Me. O My servants! If the first of you and the last of you, the humans among you and the jinn among you were as righteous as the most righteous one amongst you, this would not increase My dominion in the least. O My servants! If the first of you and the last of you, the humans among you and the jinn among you were as indecent as the most indecent one amongst you, this would not diminish My dominion in the least. O My servants! If the first of you and the last of you, your humans as well as your jinns were to stand in one plateau and make requests from Me and I were to grant each one of you his request it would diminish what I have only as a needle would diminish a sea when it is dipped into it. O My servants! They are but your works that I keep count of and then show to you. Whoever finds good, let him praise God, and whoever finds something different, let him blame no one but himself.'

[Narrated by Muslim]

His saying (*I have prohibited oppression for Myself and made it prohibited amongst you*), according to one scholar, means: it does not behove Me nor is it possible that I oppress, as God Most High says, *and it behoves not the All-Merciful to take a son* [*Maryam* 19: 92], so oppression is impossible on behalf of God Most High. One scholar said about this prophetic saying: 'It is not right for anyone to request God Most High to judge his opponent with anything except that which is right due to His words, exalted is He: "I have prohibited oppression for Myself." This is because God, may He be exalted, does not wrong His servants, so how can anybody think that He will wrong His servants for the sake of somebody else.' He also said: 'Do not wrong each other', which means that the person who wrongs someone has to be retaliated against in favour of the wronged person.

His saying (*You are all misguided except him whom I guide.... You are all naked except him whom I clothe*) is to draw our attention to our indigence and inability to procure benefits for ourselves or to drive away harm unless God, exalted is He, helps us to do so. This also harks back to the meaning of 'there is no might or strength except through God'. When the servant sees the signs of this blessing on him, he should know that it is from God and must therefore thank God Most High for it. Anything more requires more praise and thanking of God Most High.

His saying (*Seek guidance from Me, and I will guide you*) means request guidance from Me and I will guide you. The gist of this is that the servant should know that he sought guidance from his Lord and He guided him. If God were to guide him before he sought it from Him, it is not far-fetched that he would claim that he was guided because of a knowledge that he possessed.

The same applies to His saying (*You are all hungry...*), i.e., God has created all created beings in need of food, and every person who eats must be hungry until God brings his sustenance to him and fixes the tools that He has prepared for him. The possessor of wealth should not think that the sustenance that is in his hand, and which he lifts to his mouth, is provided to him by anyone else except God Most High. There is also an indication here of the proper conduct for the poor. It is as if He is saying: do not request sustenance from anyone but Me, for those from whom you request sustenance are also fed by Me. Therefore, seek sustenance from Me, and I will feed you, and God knows best.

His saying (*You err night and day*) contains such a rebuke that should put every single believer to shame. Likewise, God has created the night in order that He be obeyed and sincerely worshipped during it, such that works performed at night are often free from showing off and hypocrisy. Does the believer not feel ashamed in not spending night and day in God's obedience? This is because he is created to be visible to other people, and this is why every alert person should also obey God and refrain from displaying contravention amongst people. And how is it seemly for a believer to sin secretly and openly when God Most High has said after the above expression (*And I forgive all sins*)? God mentioned that He forgives all sins after He commanded people to seek forgiveness from Him lest someone despairs of God's mercy due to the gravity of the sins he may have committed.

His saying (*O My servants! If the first of you and the last of you, your humans and your jinn were to stand in one single plateau...*) draws people's attention to ask for great and momentous things. The person making requests should neither confine his supplications to a single matter nor select one request and leave out others for which he may also be in need. This is because that which is in God's possession never decreases and His stores shall never run out. One should not think that what God possesses can decrease by His spending from it, as the Messenger of God, God's blessings and peace be upon him, in another saying said: 'The Hand of God is always full; it never decreases due to spending at night or during the day. Can you not see that what God has spent since the creation of the heavens and earth has not diminished what is in His right Hand?'[48] The secret of this lies in the fact that His creative power is always capable of bringing things into existence; it is impossible for it to fail or to fall short, while its possibilities are infinite and beyond counting.

His saying (*only like a needle...*) is a simile intended to explain what can be physically seen by people. It means it will not diminish at all what is with God.

His saying (*There are but your works ... let him praise God*), i.e., he should not attribute his obedience and worship to himself, rather he should attribute them to God's given success and praise God for it.

Regarding His saying (*whoever finds other than that*), He did not say 'whoever finds bad', but meant whoever finds other than what is best, so let the person blame none but himself, to warn against entertaining the thought that blame should go to anyone but himself, and God knows best.

XXV

The Possessors of Great Wealth Have Taken all the Reward

عَنْ أَبِي ذَرٍّ رَضِيَ اللَّهُ عَنْهُ أَيْضًا، أَنَّ نَاسًا مِنْ أَصْحَابِ رَسُولِ اللَّهِ صَلَّى اللَّهُ عَلَيْهِ وَسَلَّمْ قَالُوا لِلنَّبِيِّ صَلَّى اللَّهُ عَلَيْهِ وَسَلَّمْ: يَا رَسُولَ اللَّهِ ذَهَبَ أَهْلُ الدُّثُورِ بِالْأُجُورِ يُصَلُّونَ كَمَا نُصَلِّي، وَيَصُومُونَ كَمَا نَصُومُ، وَيَتَصَدَّقُونَ بِفُضُولِ أَمْوَالِهِمْ. قَالَ: أَوَلَيْسَ قَدْ جَعَلَ اللَّهُ لَكُمْ مَا تَصَّدَّقُونَ؟ إِنَّ بِكُلِّ تَسْبِيحَةٍ صَدَقَةً، وَكُلِّ تَكْبِيرَةٍ صَدَقَةً، وَكُلِّ تَحْمِيدَةٍ صَدَقَةً، وَكُلِّ تَهْلِيلَةٍ صَدَقَةً، وَأَمْرٌ بِالْمَعْرُوفِ صَدَقَةٌ، وَنَهْيٌ عَنْ مُنْكَرٍ صَدَقَةٌ، وَفِي بُضْعِ أَحَدِكُمْ صَدَقَةٌ. قَالُوا: يَا رَسُولَ اللَّهِ! أَيَأْتِي أَحَدُنَا شَهْوَتَهُ وَيَكُونُ لَهُ فِيهَا أَجْرٌ؟ قَالَ: أَرَأَيْتُمْ لَوْ وَضَعَهَا فِي حَرَامٍ أَكَانَ عَلَيْهِ وِزْرٌ؟ فَكَذَلِكَ إِذَا وَضَعَهَا فِي الْحَلَالِ، كَانَ لَهُ أَجْرٌ.

رَوَاهُ مُسْلِمٌ [رقم:١٠٠٦]

On the authority of Abū Dharr, may God be well pleased with him, who reported that a group among the Companions of the Messenger of God, God's blessings and peace be upon him, said to the Prophet, God's blessings and peace be upon him: 'The possessors of wealth have taken all the rewards: they pray as we pray, fast as we fast, but give in charity the surplus of their wealth.' He said, 'Has God not made for you that which you can give in charity? Every pronouncement of "glory be to God" is a charity, every pronouncement of "God is the greatest" is a charity, every "praise be to God" is a charity, every "there is no god but God" is a charity, every enjoining of the good is a charity, every forbidding of the wrong is a charity and your conjugal relations are a charity.' They said, 'O Messenger of God! Is one of us rewarded for satisfying his sexual desire?' He said, 'Would he not incur a sin if he were to satisfy it with that which is unlawful? Likewise, he has a reward if he were to satisfy it with that which is lawful.'

[Narrated by Muslim]

This prophetic saying points to the merit of saying 'glory be to God'(*subḥān Allāh*) and other formulas of remembrance, as well as to enjoining the good and forbidding the wrong and having a good intention upon engaging in permissible things, for these become acts of obedience when sincerely intended.

There is also proof in it for the permissibility of asking questions for one who ignores the proofs given in answer to a certain question when he knows that the questioned person does not mind being asked and no ill-manners are involved in the process of asking. It also indicates the permissibility for a scholar to mention proofs in answer to intricate questions.

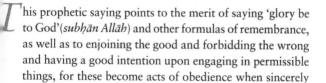

His saying (*and every enjoining of the good is a charity, and every forbidding of the wrong is a charity*) is an indication that affirms the legal ruling of charity in every instance of enjoining good and forbidding wrong is more emphasized than glorifying God or saying the other things mentioned after it. This is because enjoining good and forbidding wrong is a collective obligation and one may be called to fulfil it personally, whereas the other pronouncements of formulas of remembrance are supererogatory acts. However, the reward of obligations is greater than the reward of supererogatory acts, as indicated by God's words, 'My slave does not draw nearer to Me with better than that which I have made obligatory upon him.'[49]

As for his saying (*and your conjugal relations are a charity*), it refers to what we have said regarding permissible things turning into acts of obedience when accompanied by good intentions. Sexual intercourse becomes an act of worship when a person intends to fulfil the right of his spouse, treat her with kindness, have a righteous child, save himself and his wife from longing to have sex out of wedlock, or achieve any other good legally-countenanced objective.

Their saying (*is one of us rewarded for satisfying his sexual desire?*) and he saying (*Would he not incur a sin if he were to satisfy it with that which is unlawful?*) indicate that analogy (*qiyās*) is permissible. This is the adopted opinion of most scholars, as only the Ẓāhirites have disagreed with it.[50] As for the reported censure of analogy from the followers of the prophetic Companions and others after them, this does not relate to analogy as practised by the expert jurists, which is reverse analogy (*qiyās al-ʿaks*). The legal theorists have different opinions about using it, and this prophetic saying is a proof for those who use it in the derivation of legal rulings.

XXVI

The Merit of Reconciling People, Applying Justice and Helping them

عَنْ أَبِي هُرَيْرَةَ رَضِيَ اللهُ عَنْهُ قَالَ: قَالَ رَسُولُ اللهِ صَلَّى اللهُ عَلَيْهِ وَسَلَّمْ: كُلُّ سُلَامَىٰ مِنَ النَّاسِ عَلَيْهِ صَدَقَةٌ كُلَّ يَوْمٍ تَطْلُعُ فِيهِ الشَّمْسُ: تَعْدِلُ بَيْنَ اثْنَيْنِ صَدَقَةٌ، وَتُعِينُ الرَّجُلَ فِي دَابَّتِهِ فَتَحْمِلُهُ عَلَيْهَا أَوْ تَرْفَعُ لَهُ عَلَيْهَا مَتَاعَهُ صَدَقَةٌ، وَالْكَلِمَةُ الطَّيِّبَةُ صَدَقَةٌ، وَبِكُلِّ خُطْوَةٍ تَمْشِيهَا إِلَى الصَّلَاةِ صَدَقَةٌ، وَتُمِيطُ الْأَذَىٰ عَنِ الطَّرِيقِ صَدَقَةٌ.

رَوَاهُ الْبُخَارِيُّ [رقم:٢٩٨٩] وَمُسْلِمٌ [رقم:١٠٠٩]

On the authority of Abū Hurayrah, may God be well pleased with him, who reported that the Messenger of God, God's blessings and peace be upon him, said: 'There is in every single joint of a person an act of charity on every day that the sun rises: to reconcile two people is an act of charity; to help a man with his beast by putting him on its back or lifting his stuff onto it is an act of charity; a good word is an act of charity; every step you take on your way to the mosque is an act of charity; and removing a harmful thing from the road is an act of charity."

[Narrated by Bukhārī and Muslim]

His saying (*joints*) also includes the limbs. It is affirmed in the rigorously-authenticated collection of Muslim that the number of a person's joints is 360. Qāḍī ʿIyāḍ said, 'It originally referred to the bones of the hands and feet but later included all the bones and joints of the body.' A scholar said, 'What is meant by an "act of charity" is encouragement and warning, not obligation.' In another version of this prophetic saying narrated by Muslim the Messenger of God, God's blessings and peace be upon him, is reported to have said: 'Every joint of one of you reaches the morning with an act of charity; every glorification of God is an act of charity, every praising of God is an act of charity, every pronouncement of "there is no god but God" is an act of charity, every "God is the greatest" is an act of charity, enjoining good is an act of charity, forbidding wrong is an act of charity, [yet] two units of prayer performed at midmorning will compensate for all of that.' In other words, instead of making all these acts of remembrance as acts of charity for one's joints, it is enough to perform two units of prayer, for the prayer is an act for all the limbs of the body, and if one prays then each limb would do its duty, and God knows best.

XXVII

Piety is Good Character

عَنْ النَّوَّاسِ بْنِ سَمْعَانَ رَضِيَ اللهُ عَنْهُ عَنْ النَّبِيِّ صَلَّى اللهُ عَلَيْهِ وَسَلَّمْ قَالَ: الْبِرُّ حُسْنُ الْخُلُقِ، وَالْإِثْمُ مَا حَاكَ فِي صَدْرِكَ، وَكَرِهْتَ أَنْ يَطَّلِعَ عَلَيْهِ النَّاسُ.

رَوَاهُ مُسْلِمٌ [رقم: ٢٥٥٣]

وَعَنْ وَابِصَةَ بْنِ مَعْبَدٍ رَضِيَ اللهُ عَنْهُ قَالَ: أَتَيْتُ رَسُولَ اللهِ صَلَّى اللهُ عَلَيْهِ وَسَلَّمْ فَقَالَ: جِئْتَ تَسْأَلُ عَنْ الْبِرِّ؟ قُلْتُ: نَعَمْ. فَقَالَ: اسْتَفْتِ قَلْبَكَ، الْبِرُّ مَا اطْمَأَنَّتْ إِلَيْهِ النَّفْسُ، وَاطْمَأَنَّ إِلَيْهِ الْقَلْبُ، وَالْإِثْمُ مَا حَاكَ فِي النَّفْسِ وَتَرَدَّدَ فِي الصَّدْرِ، وَإِنْ أَفْتَاكَ النَّاسُ وَأَفْتَوْكَ.

رَوَاهُ أَحْمَد [رقم: ٤-٢٢٧] وَالدَّارِمِيّ [٢-٢٤٦]

On the authority of al-Nawwās ibn Samʿān, may God be well pleased with him, who reported that the Messenger of God, God's blessings and peace be upon him, said: 'Piety is good character and sin is what oppresses your heart and you dislike people to find out about." [Narrated by Muslim.] And on the authority of Wābiṣah ibn Maʿbad, may God be well pleased with him, who said, 'I went to see the Messenger of God, God's blessings and peace be upon him, and upon seeing me, he said: "You came to ask about piety?" I said, "Yes, indeed!" He said: "Search your heart. Piety is that which the soul finds comfort in while sin is what the soul finds repugnant and oppressive to the heart, even if people tell you again and again that it is otherwise."'

[Narrated by Aḥmad and Dārimī]

His saying, God's blessings and peace be upon him, (*piety is good character*) means that good character is the greatest characteristic of piety, which is reminiscent of his saying, God's blessings and peace be upon him: 'The pilgrimage is ʿArafah.'[51] As for piety, it is that which vindicates its doer and makes him join the ranks of the pious, or those who obey God Most High. What is meant by good character is fairness in one's dealings, kindness in one's endeavours, being just in one's judgements, giving generously, as well as other qualities of the believers whom God Most High has described by His words, *Those only are believers who, when God is mentioned, their hearts quake, and when His signs are recited to them, it increases them in faith, and in their Lord they put their trust, those who perform the prayer, and expend of what We have provided them, those in truth are the believers* [*al-Anfāl* 8: 2–4] and His words, *Those who repent, those who serve, those who pray, those who journey, those who bow, those who prostrate themselves, those who bid to honour and forbid dishonour, those who keep God's bounds – and give thou good tidings to the believers* [*al-Tawbah* 9: 112], *Prosperous are the believers who in their prayers are humble and from idle talk turn away and at almsgiving are active and guard their private parts save from their wives and what their right hands own then being not blameworthy (but whosoever seeks after more than that, those are the transgressors) and who preserve their trusts and their covenant and who observe their prayers. Those are the inheritors who shall inherit Paradise therein dwelling forever* [*al-Mu'minūn* 23: 1–10] and, *The servants of the All-Merciful are those who walk in the earth modestly* [*al-Furqān* 25: 63].

If one is unsure about his own state, let him check himself against the above Qurānic verses: to have all of these qualities is a sign of good character, and lacking all of them is a sign of bad character, while possessing some of them and lacking others indicates that one has some good character traits but lacks other ones, and one should therefore occupy oneself with preserving what one has and striving to acquire what one lacks.

However, let no one think that good character consists of only being gentle and refraining from indecent acts or acts of disobedience, and that whoever does so has refined his character. Rather, good character consists of what we have mentioned of the characteristics of the believers and assuming their character traits.

Of good character is to withstand harm from people. It is reported in the two collections of rigorously-authenticated prophetic sayings of Bukhārī and Muslim that a desert Arab pulled towards himself the mantle of the Prophet, God's blessings and peace be upon him, so hard that its edges dug marks into the shoulder of the Prophet, God's blessings and peace be upon him, upon which he said: 'O Muhammad! Order that I be given of God's wealth that you have with you.' The Messenger of God, God's blessings and peace be upon him, turned back towards the man, laughed and ordered that he be given something.

His saying (*Sin is what oppresses your heart and you dislike people to find out about*) means it is anything that creates repulsion in your heart. This is a fundamental yardstick that ought to be employed to distinguish sins from pious works. Sin is what is concocted in one's chest and one dislikes people to find out about, i.e., people of similar or better social standing, not the commonality of people. This is sin, which one should refrain from, and God knows best.

XXVIII

The Necessity of Adhering to the Prophetic Practice

عَنْ أَبِي نَجِيحٍ الْعِرْبَاضِ بْنِ سَارِيَةَ رَضِيَ اللَّهُ عَنْهُ قَالَ: وَعَظَنَا رَسُولُ اللَّهِ صَلَّى اللَّهُ عَلَيْهِ وَسَلَّمَ مَوْعِظَةً وَجِلَتْ مِنْهَا الْقُلُوبُ، وَذَرَفَتْ مِنْهَا الْعُيُونُ، فَقُلْنَا: يَا رَسُولَ اللَّهِ! كَأَنَّهَا مَوْعِظَةُ مُوَدِّعٍ فَأَوْصِنَا، قَالَ: أُوصِيكُمْ بِتَقْوَى اللَّهِ، وَالسَّمْعِ وَالطَّاعَةِ وَإِنْ تَأَمَّرَ عَلَيْكُمْ عَبْدٌ، وَإِنَّهُ مَنْ يَعِشْ مِنْكُمْ فَسَيَرَى اخْتِلَافًا كَثِيرًا، فَعَلَيْكُمْ بِسُنَّتِي وَسُنَّةِ الْخُلَفَاءِ الرَّاشِدِينَ الْمَهْدِيِّينَ، عَضُّوا عَلَيْهَا بِالنَّوَاجِذِ، وَإِيَّاكُمْ وَمُحْدَثَاتِ الْأُمُورِ فَإِنَّ كُلَّ بِدْعَةٍ ضَلَالَةٌ.

رَوَاهُ أَبُو دَاوُدَ [رقم: ٤٦٠٧] وَالتِّرْمِذِيُّ [رقم: ٢٦٧٦]

On the authority of Abū Najīḥ al-ʿIrbāḍ ibn Sāriyah, may God be well pleased with him, who said: 'The Messenger of God, God's blessings and peace be upon him, admonished us once with an eloquent admonition that filled our hearts with fear and our eyes with tears. We said: "O Messenger of God! It is as if this is an admonition of someone who is going to depart from us, so enjoin us." He said: "I enjoin you to fear God and to hear and obey even if a slave is appointed as your leader. Indeed, the one amongst you who shall live on will see a great deal of differing. Hold fast to my wont and the wont of the rightly-guided successors: hold fast to them with your teeth. Beware of matters newly begun, for every innovation is a ruinous misguidance."'

[Narrated by Abū Dāwūd and Tirmidhī]

In some other versions of this same prophetic saying it is stated: 'This is an admonition of someone who is bidding us farewell, so what do you enjoin us to do?' He said: 'I have left you upon a clear, bright way, its night like its day, and none will deviate from it except a doomed person.'

His saying (*an eloquent admonition*)[52] means one that has got to us and affected our hearts and filled them with fear, as if he wanted to make them fearful and threaten them with God's punishment in case they did not heed his admonition.

His saying (*I enjoin you to fear God and hear and obey*), i.e., those who run your affairs, even if a slave is appointed as your leader. And in some other versions of this same prophetic saying it is mentioned, 'even if an Ethiopian slave is appointed as your leader.' A scholar said: 'A slave cannot be appointed as a leader but he is used here as a supposition, though it is unlike his other saying, God's blessings and peace be upon him, "Whoever builds for the sake of God a mosque the size of a sand grouse's hole, God will build for him a house in Paradise."'[53] Now, the hole of a sand grouse cannot be a mosque, but similes contain this sort of depiction. It is also probable that the Prophet, God's blessings and peace be upon him, has been informed of the corruption of the matter [of leadership] and that it will be conferred on people who do not deserve it such that slaves are appointed as leaders. If this were ever to take place, you should hear and obey to allow the prevalence of the lesser of two evils, which is putting up with the leadership of the one whose leadership is not permissible lest resisting him leads to a greater tribulation.

His saying (*the one amongst you who shall live will see a great deal of differing*) is one of his miracles, God's blessings and peace be upon him, for he informed his Companions of what would happen after him of disagreement and the prevalence of objectionable matters. He knew what was going to happen in detail but did not convey it to everyone, preferring instead to warn against it in general terms. However, he did convey its details to a few Companions such as Ḥudhayfah ibn al-Yamān and Abū Hurayrah, which is proof of their momentous rank and status.

His saying (*Hold fast to my wont*), i.e., his clear practice [or Sunnah], (*and the wont of the rightly-guided successors*), i.e., those who are embraced by guidance, and they are four in number by consensus: Abū Bakr, ʿUmar, ʿUthmān and ʿAlī, may God be well pleased with all of them. The Prophet, God's blessings and peace be upon him, ordered to be firm on the wont of the rightly-guided successors for two reasons. Firstly, for the sake of emulation for those who are unable to look into the source-texts of the religion. Secondly, to give preponderance to their decisions and opinions when there are differences of opinion among the prophetic Companions.

As for his saying (*Beware of matters newly begun*), you should know that what is newly begun is of two types: newly-begun matters that have no foundation in the Sacred Law and these are blameworthy and void; and newly-begun matters that are weighed against similar matters, which are not blameworthy, and these [kind of newly-begun] matters are not blameworthy. This is because the terms 'innovation' and 'newly begun' are not censured simply because of the terms themselves but due to the meaning of opposition to the prophetic practice and invitation to ruinous misguidance they may connote. Otherwise, these terms should not be censured absolutely. God Most High says in the Qur'ān, *Whenever any fresh revelation comes to them from their Lord, they listen to it with amusement and frivolous hearts* [*al-Anbiyā'* 21: 2–3]. And ʿUmar, may God be well pleased with him, said: 'What a good innovation this is',[54] meaning the night prayer during the month of Ramadan (*tarāwīḥ*), and God knows best.

XXIX

What Makes One Enter Paradise

عَـنْ مُعَاذِ بْنِ جَبَلٍ رَضِيَ اللَّهُ عَنْهُ قَالَ: قُلْتُ يَا رَسُولَ اللَّهِ! أَخْبِرْنِي بِعَمَلٍ يُدْخِلُنِي الْجَنَّةَ وَيُبَاعِدُنِي مِـنَ النَّارِ، قَـالَ: لَقَدْ سَأَلْتَ عَنْ عَظِيمٍ، وَإِنَّهُ لَيَسِيرٌ عَلَىٰ مَنْ يَسَّرَهُ اللَّهُ عَلَيْهِ: تَعْبُدُ اللَّهَ لَا تُشْرِكُ بِـهِ شَيْئًا، وَتُقِيمُ الصَّلَاةَ، وَتُؤْتِي الزَّكَـاةَ، وَتَصُومُ رَمَضَانَ، وَتَحُجُّ الْبَيْتَ، ثُمَّ قَالَ: أَلَا أَدُلُّكَ عَلَىٰ أَبْوَابِ الْخَيْرِ؟ الصَّوْمُ جُنَّةٌ، وَالصَّدَقَةُ تُطْفِئُ الْخَطِيئَةَ كَمَا يُطْفِئُ الْمَاءُ النَّارَ، وَصَلَاةُ الرَّجُلِ فِي جَوْفِ اللَّيْلِ، ثُمَّ تَلَا: ﴿تَتَجَافَىٰ جُنُوبُهُمْ عَنِ الْمَضَاجِعِ﴾ حَتَّىٰ بَلَغَ ﴿... يَعْمَلُونَ﴾، ثُمَّ قَالَ: أَلَا أُخْبِرُكَ بِرَأْسِ الْأَمْرِ وَعَمُودِهِ وَذِرْوَةِ سَنَامِهِ؟ قُلْتُ: بَلَىٰ يَا رَسُولَ اللَّهِ. قَـالَ: رَأْسُ الْأَمْرِ الْإِسْلَامُ، وَعَمُودُهُ الصَّلَاةُ، وَذِرْوَةُ سَنَامِهِ الْجِهَادُ، ثُـمَّ قَـالَ: أَلَا أُخْـبِرُكَ بِـمِلَاكِ ذَٰلِكَ كُلِّهِ؟ فَقُلْـتُ: بَلَىٰ يَا رَسُولَ اللَّهِ! فَأَخَذَ بِلِسَانِهِ وَقَـالَ: كُـفَّ عَلَيْكَ هَذَا.

قُلْت: يَا نَبِيَّ اللهِ وَإِنَّا لَمُؤَاخَذُونَ بِمَا نَتَكَلَّمُ بِهِ؟ فَقَالَ: ثَكِلَتْكَ أُمُّكَ! وَهَلْ يَكُبُّ النَّاسَ عَلَى وُجُوهِهِمْ - أَوْ قَالَ عَلَى مَنَاخِرِهِمْ - إِلَّا حَصَائِدُ أَلْسِنَتِهِمْ!

رَوَاهُ التِّرْمِذِيُّ [رقم: ٢٦١٦]

On the authority of Muʿādh ibn Jabal, may God be well pleased with him, who said, 'I said, "O Messenger of God! Tell me about a work that will enter me into Paradise and distance me from the Fire." He said: "You have asked about a tremendous thing, and verily it is easy for whomever God has made it easy. Adore God and do not associate any partner with Him, establish the prayer, pay the poor-due, fast the month of Ramadan and make the pilgrimage to God's House." Then he said, "Shall I not inform you about the doors of all good? Fasting is a shield, the act of charity puts out sin like water puts out fire, and the man's prayer in the middle of the night." Then he recited the words of God, *Their sides shun their couches as they call on their Lord in fear and hope; and they expend of that We have provided them. No soul knows what comfort is laid up for them secretly, as a recompense for that they were doing* [*al-Sajdah* 32: 16–17]. Then he said, "Shall I not inform you about the matter's apex, buttress and summit?" I said, "Yes, indeed, O Messenger of God!" He said, "The apex of the matter is Islam, its buttress is the prayer and its summit is jihad." Then he said, "Shall I not inform you about the essential prerequisite of all that?" I said, "Yes, indeed, O Messenger of God!" He grabbed his tongue and said, "Hold this back." I said, "Are we taken to task for what we say?" He said: "May your mother be bereft of you! Are people thrown on their faces – or he said: their nostrils – into the Fire except for what their tongues have reaped?"'

[Narrated by Tirmidhī]

His saying (*You have asked about a tremendous thing, and verily it is easy for whomever God has made it easy*) means that for whom God has given success to be guided, and then directed to worship Him sincerely without associating anyone or anything with Him. Then he said (*establish the prayer*), i.e., perform it in the most perfect manner. And then he mentioned the prescriptions of Islam: the poor-due, fasting and the pilgrimage. After which he said, (*Shall I not inform you about the doors of all good? Fasting is a shield*), by which he meant fasting outside of Ramadan, for the latter had already been mentioned. What is emphasized here is abundant fasting for it is a shield, i.e., a protection and cover from the Fire.

Then he said (*The act of charity puts out sin...*) meaning here charity other than the poor-due (*zakāh*). (*And the man's prayer in the middle of the night*), and then he recited the words of God Most High, *Their sides shun their couches as they call on their Lord in fear and hope; and they expend of that We have provided them. No soul knows what comfort is laid up for them secretly, as a recompense for that they were doing* [*al-Sajdah* 32: 16–17]), which means whoever wakes up in the middle of the night, leaves his sleep and desire, preferring instead what he hopes for from God, his reward will be that which is mentioned in the Qurānic verse, *No soul knows what comfort is laid up for them secretly, as a recompense for that they were doing* [*al-Sajdah* 32: 17].[55] It is reported in one tradition that 'God takes pride in the person who stands to pray at night, saying [to the angels]: "Look at My servants, how they got up in the dead of night where none sees them but I. I take you as witnesses that I have granted them the abode of My favour."'

Then he said (*Shall I not inform you about the matter's apex ... its buttress is the prayer*): the buttress of a thing is that which makes it erect, such that there is usually no firmness without a buttress. And his saying (*its summit is jihad*) is because no other work compares with jihad, as reported by Abū Hurayrah: 'A man came to the Messenger of God, God's blessings and peace be upon him, and said: "Guide me to a work equivalent to jihad." He said: "I cannot think of one." Then he said: "When the fighter goes out, can you enter your mosque and pray non-stop and fast non-stop?" The man said: "And who can manage that?"'[56]

His saying (*'Shall I not inform you of the essential prerequisite of all that?' I said, 'Yes, indeed, O Messenger of God!' He grabbed his tongue and said, 'Hold this back.'*) means he first prompted him to fight unbelief, then he led him to the greatest jihad which is fighting the ego and forcing it to cease talking about that which harms and ruins it. This is because he attributed the reason for people being thrown on their faces in the Fire, in most cases, to their tongues. The prophetic saying narrated by Bukhārī and Muslim has already been mentioned: 'Whoever believes in God and the Last Day, let him say something good or else keep quiet,' and in another prophetic saying, 'Whoever guarantees for me [i.e. to keep away from the unlawful] what is between his jawbones and legs, I will guarantee for him Paradise.'[57]

XXX

The Rights of God Most High

عَنْ أَبِي ثَعْلَبَةَ الْخُشَنِيِّ جُرْثُومِ بن نَاشِرٍ رَضِيَ اللَّهُ عَنْهُ عَـنْ رَسُولِ اللَّهِ صَلَّى اللَّهُ عَلَيْهِ وَسَلَّمْ قَالَ: إِنَّ اللَّهَ تَعَالَى فَرَضَ فَرَائِضَ فَلَا تُضَيِّعُوهَا، وَحَدَّ حُدُودًا فَلَا تَعْتَدُوهَا، وَحَرَّمَ أَشْيَاءَ فَلَا تَنْتَهِكُوهَا، وَسَكَتَ عَـنْ أَشْيَاءَ رَحْمَةً لَكُمْ غَيْرَ نِسْيَانٍ فَلَا تَبْحَثُوا عَنْهَا.

رَوَاهُ الدَّارَقُطْنِيّ [٤-١٨٤]

On the authority of Abū Thaʿlabah al-Khushanī Jurthūm ibn Nāshir, may God be well pleased with him, who reported that the Messenger of God, God's blessings and peace be upon him, said: 'God Most High has obligated some obligatory works, so do not squander them; He set boundaries, so do not transgress them; He prohibited things, so do not violate them; and He kept silent about certain things out of mercy for you, not out of forgetfulness, so do not explore them.'

[Narrated by al-Dāraquṭnī]

His saying (*do not transgress them*) means do not engage in them. As for the prohibition of investigating what God has kept silent about, this agrees with the words of the Prophet, God's blessings and peace be upon him, 'Leave me alone for as long as I leave you alone, for those before you were not destroyed except for their excessive questioning and opposition to their prophets.'[58] A scholar said: 'The Children of Israel used to ask questions and receive answers, they were granted whatever they requested until this became a trial for them which led to their destruction.'

The prophetic Companions, may God be well pleased with them, understood this danger and, therefore, refrained from asking questions except in matters that were necessary. This is also why they liked the visits of the Bedouins who came to ask questions of the Messenger, God's blessings and peace be upon him; they listened to the answers given and understood their implications.

Some have exaggerated the matter and claimed that it is impermissible to ask the scholars about momentous and serious events until these actually happen. The pious Predecessors used to say about such momentous events, 'Do not enquire about them until they take place.' However, when the scholars feared the disappearance of knowledge, they laid down legal principles and derived legal details from them, just as they anticipated the advent of events and questions, and wrote about their appropriate solutions.

The scholars also differ about the legal rulings of things prior to the pronouncement of the Sacred Law: are they to be considered unlawful, permissible, or should judgement be suspended about them? There are three different opinions about this, all of which are mentioned in the books of legal theory.

Genuine Non-Attachment

عَنْ أَبِي الْعَبَّاسِ سَهْلِ بْنِ سَعْدٍ السَّاعِدِيِّ رَضِيَ اللَّهُ عَنْهُ قَالَ:
جَاءَ رَجُلٌ إِلَى النَّبِيِّ صَلَّى اللَّهُ عَلَيْهِ وَسَلَّمَ فَقَالَ: يَا رَسُولَ
اللَّهِ، دُلَّنِي عَلَى عَمَلٍ إِذَا عَمِلْتُهُ أَحَبَّنِي اللَّهُ وَأَحَبَّنِي النَّاسُ.
فَقَالَ: ازْهَدْ فِي الدُّنْيَا يُحِبَّكَ اللَّهُ، وَازْهَدْ فِيمَا عِنْدَ النَّاسِ
يُحِبَّكَ النَّاسُ.

رَوَاهُ مُسْلِمٌ

On the authority of Abū'l-ʿAbbās Sahl ibn Saʿd al-Sāʿidī, may
God be well pleased with him, who reported that a man came to
the Prophet, God's blessings and peace be upon him, and said: 'O
Messenger of God, tell me about an act that, if I were to perform
it, God will love me and people will also love me.' He said, 'Be
unattached to this world, and God will love you; and be unattached to what people possess and they will love you.'

[Narrated by Muslim]

Know that the Messenger of God, God's blessings and peace
be upon him, has encouraged us to possess little of this

world and to be unattached to it. He said, 'Be in this world like a stranger or a traveller passing through',[59] and he also said, 'Love of this world is the beginning of every sin',[60] and in another saying he said, 'The person who is unattached to this world puts his heart at rest in this world and in the next, while the one who desires this world tires his heart in this world and in the next.'[61]

You should also know that one is a guest is in this world and that whatever is in one's hand is borrowed; the guest must surely leave at some point of time and what is borrowed has to be given back eventually. 'This world is a fleeting accident from which both the pious and the profligate feed.'[62] It is made abhorrent to the friend of God but beloved to its folk. Whoever shares with the folk of this world what is beloved to them will certainly be despised by them.

The Messenger of God, God's blessings and peace be upon him, directed the questioner to forgo this world by being unattached to it, promising him the love of God, i.e. His good pleasure, if he did so. This is because God's love of His servants is tantamount to His good pleasure with them. The Prophet, God's blessings and peace be upon him, also directed the questioner to be unattached to what is in people's possession if he wanted people to love him. Wealth amounts to love of this world, for there is nothing in people's possession about which they do compete and because of which they despise one another except this world.

The Messenger of God, God's blessings and peace be upon him, said, 'Whoever makes the Afterlife his only concern, God will concentrate his focus, put richness in his heart and this world will come to him willy-nilly. And whoever makes this world his only concern, God will disperse his focus, put poverty before his eyes and, ultimately, he will not obtain anything from this world except that which has been destined for him. Indeed, felicitous is he who prefers a permanent abode whose bounties are everlasting over an evanescent abode whose chastisement is ever unceasing.'[63]

XXXII

No Harm and No Reciprocating Harm

عَنْ أَبِي سَعِيدٍ - سَعْدِ بْنِ سِنَانٍ - الْخُدْرِيِّ رَضِيَ اللهُ عَنْهُ أَنَّ رَسُولَ اللهِ صَلَّى اللهُ عَلَيْهِ وَسَلَّمْ قَالَ: لَا ضَرَرَ وَلَا ضِرَارَ.

رَوَاهُ ابْنُ مَاجَهْ [رقم: ٢٣٤١] وَالدَّارَقُطْنِيّ [رقم: ٤-٢٢٨] وَمَالِكٌ [٢-٧٤٦]

On the authority of Abū Saʿīd Saʿd ibn Sinān al-Khudrī, may God be well pleased with him, that the Messenger of God, God's blessings and peace be upon him, said, 'No harm and no reciprocating harm.'

[Narrated by Ibn Mājah, Dāraquṭnī and Mālik]

You should know that whoever harms his brother has wronged him, and wronging him is prohibited as already pointed out in the Prophetic saying reported by Abū Dharr, 'O My servants! I have prohibited oppression for Myself, and made it prohibited amongst you, so do not oppress one another.'[64] The Prophet, God's blessings and peace be upon him, also said: 'Your lives, properties and honour are unlawful for you [to violate].'[65]

Ibn Ḥabīb wrote, '"No harm" means to let no one bring about harm to any person who has not brought it on himself. And "no reciprocating harm" means that no one should be harmed because of somebody else.' Al-Muḥsinī said, 'Harm is that in which there is benefit for one and detriment for one's neighbour.' Another scholar said: '"No harm and no reciprocating harm" means that no harm should be inflicted on those who have not harmed one just as no harm should be inflicted on those who have harmed one. This is like the saying of the Prophet, God's blessings and peace be upon him: "Hand over the trust to the one who entrusted you with it and do not betray him who betrays you."'[66] The meaning of the last Prophetic saying according to one scholar is: do not betray the person who betrays you after getting the upper hand over him regarding his betrayal. It is as if the prohibition here relates to the initiation of the act. As for the person who retaliates with the like of what has been inflicted on him and regains his right, such a person is not traitorous. Rather, the traitor is he who takes what is not his or more than what is due to him.

The jurists differ amongst themselves regarding a person who denies a right due on him but whose property then falls into the hands of the person whose right is denied, through being entrusted with this wealth or the like. One scholar was of the opinion that it is not permissible for him to take his right because of the outward purport of the saying of the Prophet, God's blessings and peace be upon him, 'Hand over the trust to him who entrusted you with it and do not betray those who betray you.' Others stated that it is allowed for him to vindicate himself and take his right from the wealth in his hand. The evidence for their opinion is the saying reported by ʿĀ'ishah about the story of Hind with Abū Sufyān.[67] Regarding this question, the jurists have different considerations and ways of understanding the implications derived from this saying, but this is not the place to mention all of them. What seems to be correct in this context is that a person is not allowed to harm his brother whether the latter has harmed him or not. However, he can retaliate and punish anyone who harms him, if he is able to do so, within the limits of what is permissible for him. This is not oppression, nor is it inflicting harm if it is carried out in the manner made permissible by the Sunnah.

Shaykh Abū ʿAmr ibn al-Ṣalāḥ, may God have mercy on him, said, 'This prophetic saying came down to us through different chains of transmission which when taken together make this saying strong and authenticated. The majority of scholars have transmitted it and used it as a legal proof. Abū Dāwūd is reported as saying, "Jurisprudence revolves around five Prophetic sayings" and he mentioned the above one amongst them.'

XXXIII

A Claimant Must Present his Proof and the One who Denies his Claim must Take an Oath

عَنْ ابْنِ عَبَّاسٍ رَضِيَ اللّٰهُ عَنْهُمَا أَنَّ رَسُولَ اللّٰهِ صَلَّى اللّٰهُ عَلَيْهِ وَسَلَّمْ قَالَ: لَوْ يُعْطَى النَّاسُ بِدَعْوَاهُمْ لَادَّعَى رِجَالٌ أَمْوَالَ قَوْمٍ وَدِمَاءَهُمْ، لَكِنِ الْبَيِّنَةُ عَلَى الْمُدَّعِي، وَالْيَمِينُ عَلَى مَنْ أَنْكَرَ.

رَوَاهُ الْبَيْهَقِيّ [١٠-٢٥٢]

On the authority of Ibn ʿAbbās, may God be well pleased with father and son, who reported that the Messenger of God, God's blessings and peace be upon him, said: 'Were people to be given on the basis of their claims, some men would claim the wealth and lives of other people. Rather, proof is required from whoever makes a claim, and an oath from whoever denies it.'

[Narrated by al-Bayhaqī]

The version which is in the rigorously-authenticated collections of Bukhārī and Muslim is reported on the authority of Ibn Abī Malīkah who said, 'Ibn ʿAbbās, may God be well pleased with father and son, wrote that the Prophet, God's blessings and peace be upon him, decreed that an oath is required from the person against whom a claim is made.' And in another version, the Prophet, God's blessings and peace be upon him, said, 'Were people to be given on the basis of their claims, some men would claim the wealth and lives of other men. Rather, the person against whom a claim is made must make an oath [that the claim is false].'[68]

This prophetic saying is one of the principles of legal prescriptions, and the greatest point of reference regarding people's disputes and contentions. It requires that judgement is not made in favour of anyone on the sole basis of his claim.

His saying (*some men would claim the wealth and lives of other people*) is taken as evidence by some scholars for the invalidity of Imām Mālik's opinion, which states that one must accept the words of the murdered person who proclaims [just before giving up the ghost] that 'So-and-so has killed me' or 'My blood is on so-and-so'. For if the words of a sick person who says 'so-and-so owes me a piece of gold or silver' are not accepted at face value, it is more appropriate not to accept the words of someone who claims that his blood is on such-and-such a person. However, their argument against Mālik does not stand, for he did not base retaliatory punishments or blood money on the words of the claimant, but rather on swearing an oath on murder. Moreover, he understands the words of the murdered person, 'my blood is on so-and-so' to be the witness on oath of one person, which strengthens the proof of the claimant until those against whom the claim is made are proven innocent through making an oath in cases such as this one.

Regarding his saying (*Rather, the person against whom a claim is made must make an oath*), the scholars are unanimous that the person against whom a claim is made must take an oath if the claim in question relates to property. When it does not relate to property, their opinions differ. Some of them were of the opinion that an oath is obligatory upon any person against whom a claim is made regarding any right, divorce, marriage or freeing slaves, following the apparent general applicability of the prophetic saying. If he fails to do so, the claimant makes an oath and his claim is then affirmed. Abū Ḥanīfah, may God have mercy on him, said, 'An oath is taken when it is a question of divorce, marriage or freeing slaves. If a person fails to take the oath, the claims against him are confirmed. However, an oath is not required from a person against whom a claim is made if fixed punitive measures are involved.'

XXXIV

Forbidding the Wrong is Part of Faith

عَنْ أَبِي سَعِيدٍ الْخُدْرِيِّ رَضِيَ اللهُ عَنْهُ قَالَ: سَمِعْتُ رَسُولَ اللهِ صَلَّى اللهُ عَلَيْهِ وَسَلَّمَ يَقُولُ: مَنْ رَأَى مِنْكُمْ مُنْكَرًا فَلْيُغَيِّرْهُ بِيَدِهِ، فَإِنْ لَمْ يَسْتَطِعْ فَبِلِسَانِهِ، فَإِنْ لَمْ يَسْتَطِعْ فَبِقَلْبِهِ، وَذَلِكَ أَضْعَفُ الْإِيمَانِ.

رَوَاهُ مُسْلِمٌ [رقم:٤٩]

On the authority of Abū Saʿīd al-Khudrī, may God be well pleased with him, who said, 'I heard the Messenger of God, may God's blessings and peace be upon him, say: "Whoever sees a wrong let him change it with his hands; and if he cannot do so, then with his tongue; and if he cannot do so, then with his heart, and that is the weakest manifestation of faith."'

[Narrated by Muslim]

Muslim has also narrated this prophetic saying on the authority of Ṭāriq ibn Shihāb who said, 'The first person to start with the sermon of Eid before the prayer is Marwān [ibn al-Ḥakam]. A man stood up and said, "The prayer should be before the sermon." So he said, "This is a Sunnah that the people have already abandoned!" Abū Saᶜīd said, "This man has discharged his duty. I heard the Messenger of God, God's blessings and peace be upon him, say: 'Whoever sees a wrong, let him change it....'"'

There is in this prophetic saying proof that none did such an act before Marwān. If it were to be said, 'How is it that Abū Saᶜīd was tardy in changing this wrong such that this man was the first to object to it?' The answer would be: it is possible that Abū Saᶜīd was not present when Marwān was about to start his sermon and that the man hastened to object, upon which Abū Saᶜīd entered the mosque while the man was still talking to Marwān. It is also likely that he was present but was fearful that if he were to change the wrong a greater sedition would ensue because of his objection, and so objecting to this wrong was not obligated on him as far as this instance was concerned. It is also possible that Abū Saᶜīd was about to object when this man voiced his objection and then Abū Saᶜīd supported him, and God knows best. It is also mentioned in another prophetic saying, which was narrated by Bukhārī and Muslim and which they both placed in the rubric on the prayer of the two ᶜĪds, that it was Abū Saᶜīd who pulled Marwān by the hand when he was about to climb the pulpit. Marwān gave him the same answer that he gave the man mentioned above. It is therefore possible that these are two separate events.

As for his saying (*let him change it*), this is a command that denotes obligation by the consensus of the Muslim community. The Qur'ān and the prophetic Practice both agree about the obligation of enjoining good and forbidding wrong; it is part of doing well by the Muslims, which is a very important aspect of the religion of Islam. As for the words of God, *look after your own souls. He who is astray cannot hurt you* [*al-Mā'idah* 5: 105], these do not contradict what we have mentioned. This is because the correct meaning of this Qurānic verse according to the expert scholars is: if you do what has been made incumbent upon you, the slackness of others will not harm you. It is like His words, *no soul laden bears the load of another* [*al-Anʿām* 6: 164]. If this is the case, then one of the things that have been made incumbent upon Muslims is to enjoin good and forbid wrong. If one does so and the addressee does not comply, one does not bear that burden for one is only required to enjoin good and forbid wrong, and not to effect compliance, and God knows best.

Moreover, enjoining good and forbidding wrong is a collective obligation, so if it is done by some then others do not have to do it; yet if it is abandoned by all, then every single person who is able to do it, and who has no excuse for not doing it, will be sinful. There may also be instances whereby one is personally required to enjoin good and forbid wrong, such as when the latter is in a location that nobody knows about except him, or when no one can do it except him, or when one sees one's spouse, children or servants engage in wrongdoing and one fails to change it.

The scholars have stated that enjoining good and forbidding wrong is not forfeited because one thinks it will not be accepted by the addressee, rather one should do it regardless of whether one thinks it shall be accepted or not. God Most High says, *And remind; the Reminder profits the believers* [*al-Dhāriyāt* 51:55], *It is only for the Messenger to deliver the manifest Message* [*al-Nūr* 24: 54].

The scholars state that it is not a condition that the person who enjoins good and forbids wrong be perfect in his state, such that he complies with what he commands others to do and refrains from what he forbids them. Rather he should enjoin good and forbid wrong even if he does not practise what he preaches. This is because every person has two duties: he has to enjoin himself to do good and refrain from wrong, and he has to enjoin others to do good and refrain from wrong. If one does one of the two duties, the other remains unfulfilled. Enjoining good and forbidding wrong is not confined to those in authority. It is rather obligated on individual Muslims. However, one who does so must be knowledgeable about what is enjoined and forbidden. If it is something obvious, such as the prayer, fasting, fornication, or the consumption of alcoholic drinks, then all Muslims know these. If it is something relating to intricate statements or actions or involving legal expertise, which the generality of Muslims do not have, then they do not have to get involved in it, as this is left to the scholars. The scholars object only to that about which there is consensus. As for questions about which there is a difference of opinion, there is no objection in such cases. For according to one opinion, which is the correct position adopted by numerous expert scholars, every qualified scholar who exerts a well-considered effort to deduce a legal ruling is correct. And according to the other opinion, there is only one correct, deducted ruling, but one does not know who is the scholar with the incorrect point of view, and, in any case, there is no sin upon the latter. However, by way of doing well by others and shunning differences of opinion, it is recommended to proceed with the matter in a spirit of kindness and gentleness.

Shaykh Muḥyī al-Dīn al-Nawawī, may God have mercy on him, said, 'And know that the subject of enjoining good and forbidding wrong has been neglected in its greater part for a long time. Nowadays, only a few forms of it are still in place. But one must know that it is a tremendous domain upon which stands the whole matter [of Islam]: when wrong is abundant, punishment descends on both the righteous and the wicked. If the oppressor is not stopped, God may send his punishment on all. God Most High says, *so let those who go against His command beware, lest a trial befall them, or there befall them a painful chastisement* [*al-Nūr* 24: 63]. The seeker of the Afterlife and the person who strives to gain God's good pleasure must pay attention to this rubric, for its benefit is great, especially as most of it is gone. One should not fear those who rebuke one for enjoining good and forbidding wrong, due to their high worldly position, for God Most High says, *Assuredly God will help him who helps Him* [*al-Ḥajj* 22: 40]. Know also that the reward is commensurate with toil. One must not abstain from enjoining good and forbidding wrong due to friendship or love, for one's real friend is the one who strives to work for his Afterlife, even if this means losing out on this world. On the other hand, one's enemy is the one who strives to ruin his Afterlife, even if this results in some benefit in this world.'

The person who enjoins good and forbids wrong must exercise gentleness, for this is more likely to have an effect. Imām Shāfiʿī, may God be well pleased with him, said, 'Whoever admonishes his brother far from other people has done well by him and added to his perfections, and whoever admonishes his brother in front of others has opposed and shamed him.' Among the things that people take lightly in this domain is when they see a person selling goods or animals that have defects that he does not disclose, but they neither object nor inform any would-be buyer of these defects, when they are responsible for doing so, for the religion consists of doing well by others and whoever does not do well by others has cheated them.

As for his saying (*If he cannot do so, then with his heart*), this does not involve removing the wrong or changing it, but it is all that one can do. His saying (*and this is the weakest manifestation of faith*) means, and God knows best, faith's least of fruits. The person who enjoins good and forbids wrong does not have to search, pry, spy or break into houses on the basis of conjecture. Rather, if he comes across a wrong he should change it. Al-Māwardī said, 'One does not have to break into houses or spy unless, for example, a trustworthy person informs him that a man is alone with another man and intends to kill him, or with another woman and intends to fornicate with her. It is permissible for him in such cases to spy, investigate and enquire for fear of missing what cannot be rectified.'

There is another version of this prophetic saying in which it is stated, 'There is not after that the equivalent of a speck of faith',[69] i.e., there remains no rank of faith beneath this. It is to be noted that the meaning of faith here is Islam. There is also in this prophetic saying proof that whoever is afraid of being killed or beaten up, changing what is wrong is excused in his case. This is the adopted opinion of the expert scholars among the pious Predecessors and those who came after them. A group of immoderate scholars stated that enjoining good and forbidding wrong is not forfeited even in cases such as these.

XXXV

The Brotherhood of Islam

عَنْ أَبِي هُرَيْرَةَ رَضِيَ اللَّهُ عَنْهُ قَالَ: قَالَ رَسُولُ اللهِ صَلَّى اللهُ عَلَيْهِ وَسَلَّمَ: لَا تَحَاسَدُوا، وَلَا تَنَاجَشُوا، وَلَا تَبَاغَضُوا، وَلَا تَدَابَرُوا، وَلَا يَبِعْ بَعْضُكُمْ عَلَى بَيْعِ بَعْضٍ، وَكُونُوا عِبَادَ اللهِ إِخْوَانًا. الْمُسْلِمُ أَخُو الْمُسْلِمِ، لَا يَظْلِمُهُ، وَلَا يَخْذُلُهُ، وَلَا يَكْذِبُهُ، وَلَا يَحْقِرُهُ، التَّقْوَى هَاهُنَا، وَيُشِيرُ إِلَى صَدْرِهِ ثَلَاثَ مَرَّاتٍ، بِحَسْبِ امْرِئٍ مِنَ الشَّرِّ أَنْ يَحْقِرَ أَخَاهُ الْمُسْلِمَ، كُلُّ الْمُسْلِمِ عَلَى الْمُسْلِمِ حَرَامٌ: دَمُهُ وَمَالُهُ وَعِرْضُهُ.

رَوَاهُ مُسْلِمٌ [رقم: ٢٥٦٤]

On the authority of Abū Hurayrah, may God be well pleased with him, who reported that the Messenger of God, God's blessings and peace be upon him, said: 'Do not be resentfully envious of one another, do not artificially inflate prices against one another, do not loathe one another, do not give a cold shoulder to one another, do not undercut one another in business transactions, but be, servants of God, brothers. The Muslim is the brother of his fellow Muslim: he does not wrong him, let him down, give the lie to him or look down on him. Godfearingness is here – and he pointed to his chest three times. It is evil enough for a man to look down on his fellow Muslim! A Muslim for another Muslim is entirely inviolable: in his life, property and honour.'

[Narrated by Muslim]

In his saying (*Do not be resentfully envious of one another*), resentful envy consists of wishing the cessation of blessings for someone. Such a wish is unlawful. In another Prophetic saying, the Prophet, God's blessings and peace be upon him, said, 'Beware of resentful envy, for resentful envy consumes good deeds like fire consumes firewood or dry grass.'[70] As for appreciative envy (*ghibṭah*), it is wanting to have what the envied person has without wishing for the cessation of what he has. Sometimes when envy is mentioned in prophetic sayings, it refers to appreciative rather than resentful envy, as is in the saying of the Prophet, God's blessings and peace be upon him, 'There is no envy except in two things…',[71] i.e., there is no appreciative envy except in two things.

His saying (*do not artificially inflate prices against one another*) is because this involves cheating.

His saying (*do not loathe one another*) means do not engage in matters which may cause you to loathe one another, for love or hatred are inward states of the heart that man does not have the power to acquire or control, as the Prophet, God's blessings and peace be upon him, said, 'O God! This is my apportioning of that which I have control over, do not take me to task over that which I have no control',[72] i.e., his heart.

His saying (*do not undercut one another in business transactions*) means to say to the buyer of the merchandise during the interval during which he can return it back, 'Cancel this transaction and I will sell you the same merchandise or something better for the same price'; or the seller and the buyer may have already agreed on the price and nothing remains except sealing the contract when another seller suggests to the buyer to sell him the same merchandise for less. Once the price between the buyer and seller is fixed and agreed upon, it is prohibited for somebody else to undercut the deal. As for when the price is not agreed between the buyer and the seller, such an action is not unlawful.

The meaning of (*but be, servants of God, brothers*) is that you should interact and deal with one another the way that blood brothers deal and interact with one another, i.e., with love, kindness, pity, amiability and helping one another in acts of goodness, while, at the same time, having pure hearts towards them and doing well by them in all circumstances.

Concerning his saying (*The Muslim is the brother of his fellow Muslim: he does not wrong him, let him down, give the lie to him or look down on him*), letting him down means if a Muslim asks another Muslim to help him stop an oppressor, or something similar, it is incumbent on him to help if he is in a position to do so and does not have an excuse that is countenanced by the Sacred Law.

His saying (*Godfearingness is here – and he pointed to his chest three times...*) and, in another narration, 'God does not look at your bodies or forms, but He looks at your hearts' means that outward works do not produce Godfearingness. What brings about Godfearingness is what strikes the heart of God's immensity, fear, vigilance and gaze that encompasses all things. What this prophetic saying means, and God knows best, is that a person's reward or punishment is only according to what is in his heart, and that it is the heart that is taken into consideration.

In his saying (*It is evil enough for a man to look down on his fellow Muslim*), there is a great warning against looking down on anyone, for God Most High did not look down on him when he created him. He rather provided his sustenance, perfected his creation and subjugated everything in the heavens and earth for his sake. And although all of that is for him and others as well, at least he has a share in it. Moreover, God Most High called him 'Muslim', 'believer' and 'slave'. Not only that but He sent Muhammad, God's blessings and peace be upon him, as His Messenger to him. So whoever looks down on any Muslim has looked down on that which God Most High has exalted. To look down on another Muslim, it is enough to pass by him and neither address him with the greeting of peace nor respond to his greeting when he hastens to greet one first. Another facet of looking down on others is to deem them undeserving of entering Paradise or being saved from the Fire.

As for that which the intelligent person despises in the ignoramus, or the upright person in those who are profligate, this is not considered contempt towards other Muslims. It is rather contempt towards the quality of ignorance that the ignoramus has, or towards the characteristic of profligacy that those who are profligate have. When the ignoramus gets rid of his ignorance or the one who is profligate abandons his profligacy, he will celebrate them again and treat their high rank with deference.

XXXVI

The Merit of Gathering to Recite the Qur'ān and for Remembrance

عَنْ أَبِي هُرَيْرَةَ رَضِيَ اللَّهُ عَنْهُ عَنْ النَّبِيِّ صَلَّى اللَّهُ عَلَيْهِ وَسَلَّمْ قَالَ: مَنْ نَفَّسَ عَنْ مُؤْمِنٍ كُرْبَةً مِنْ كُرَبِ الدُّنْيَا نَفَّسَ اللَّهُ عَنْهُ كُرْبَةً مِنْ كُرَبِ يَوْمِ الْقِيَامَةِ، وَمَنْ يَسَّرَ عَلَى مُعْسِرٍ، يَسَّرَ اللَّهُ عَلَيْهِ فِي الدُّنْيَا وَالآخِرَةِ، وَمَنْ سَتَرَ مُسْلِما سَتَرَهُ اللهُ فِي الدُّنْيَا وَالآخِرَةِ، وَاللَّهُ فِي عَوْنِ الْعَبْدِ مَا كَانَ الْعَبْدُ فِي عَوْنِ أَخِيهِ، وَمَنْ سَلَكَ طَرِيقًا يَلْتَمِسُ فِيهِ عِلْمًا سَهَّلَ اللَّهُ لَهُ بِهِ طَرِيقًا إِلَى الْجَنَّةِ، وَمَا اجْتَمَعَ قَوْمٌ فِي بَيْتٍ مِنْ بُيُوتِ اللَّهِ يَتْلُونَ كِتَابَ اللَّهِ، وَيَتَدَارَسُونَهُ بَيْنَهُمْ إِلَّا نَزَلَتْ عَلَيْهِمْ السَّكِينَةُ، وَغَشِيَتْهُمْ الرَّحْمَةُ، وَحَفَّتْهُمْ الْمَلَائِكَةُ، وَذَكَرَهُمْ اللَّهُ فِيمَنْ عِنْدَهُ، وَمَنْ بَطَّأَ بِهِ عَمَلُهُ لَمْ يُسْرِعْ بِهِ نَسَبُهُ.

رواهُ مُسْلِمٌ [رقم: ٢٦٩٩]

On the authority of Abū Hurayrah, may God be well pleased with him, who reported that the Prophet, God's blessings and peace be upon him, said, 'Whoever relieves a believer from distress in this world, God will relieve him from distress on the Day of Judgement. And whoever is lenient with a person in straitened circumstances, God will be lenient with him in this world and the next. And whoever conceals a Muslim's faults, God will conceal his faults in this world and the next. And God aids the servant as long as the servant aids his brother. And whoever treads a path seeking knowledge therein, God will make easy for him a path to Paradise. And no group of people gather in one of God's houses, reciting God's Book and studying it amongst themselves, except that tranquillity descends upon them, mercy overspreads them, the angels surround them and God mentions them to those near Him. And whoever is slowed down by his works, his lineage will not make him go fast.'

[Narrated by Muslim]

This is a great prophetic saying which combines all kinds of knowledge, rules and good manners. It includes the merit of fulfilling the needs of the Muslims and benefiting them with whatever is in one's ability in terms of knowledge, wealth, assistance, directing them to an interest of theirs or simply by giving them advice and doing well by them.

His saying (*Whoever conceals a Muslim's faults*) means conceals his slips. What is meant here is concealing the faults of decent people who are not known for corruption. Moreover, such concealment relates to contraventions that have already taken place and are no longer extant. As for when one finds out about a person's contraventions and catches him in the act, then he must hasten to rebuke him and stop him from committing it. If he fails to do so, he should report the matter to the authorities when this does not lead to another act of corruption. As for the person who is known for his moral corruption, one should not conceal his faults, for doing so will embolden him to commit more acts of corruption, harm and violation of that which is unlawful. Concealing the faults of such a person will also incite others to do the same. In fact, it is recommended that one reports such a person to the authorities when one does not fear that reporting him will cause another act of corruption. The same applies to the disparagement of the narrators, witnesses and trustees of charities, endowments, orphans and the like. One must speak against others when needed and it is not permitted to conceal their slips if one sees in them something that infringes upon their suitability for the job. This is not an engagement in backbiting, which is forbidden, but rather a part of doing well by others, which is obligatory.

His saying (*And God aids the servant as long as the servant aids his brother*) is a summation that is not easy to explain. However, part of this is that when a servant decides to help his brother, he should not shrink from making a statement or declaring the truth out of faith that God will help him. This prophetic saying also includes the merit of being lenient with someone in financial hardship, as well as the merit of striving in the pursuit of knowledge. And what this implies is the merit of occupying oneself with know- ledge, i.e., sacred knowledge. But this is conditioned on seeking God's countenance in the pursuit of sacred learning, even though this is a condition in all acts of worship.

His saying, God's blessings and peace be upon him, (*And no group of people gather in one of God's houses, reciting God's Book and studying it amongst themselves*) is a proof for the merit of gathering in the mosque to recite the Qur'ān.

His saying (*And no group of people…*) means absolutely any group of people who gather for the purpose of reciting the Qur'ān in the mosque will have the same merit. The Prophet, God's blessings and peace be upon him, did not stipulate that they be scholars, ascetics or people of spiritual stations.

(*The angels surround them*), means that they sit at the edge of the gathering, as in God's saying, *And you shall see the angels encircling about the Throne* [*al-Zumar* 39: 75], i.e., encompassing the gathering and surrounding its sides. It is as if the angels are so close to them that they surround them in order not to leave any gaps for the Devil.

His saying (*and mercy overspreads them*) means covers them in their entirety.

His saying (*And God mentions them to those near Him*) requires that God Most High mentions them to the prophets and the noble angels, and God knows best.

XXXVII

The Favour and Mercy
of God Most High

عَنِ ابْنِ عَبَّاسٍ رَضِيَ اللَّهُ عَنْهُمَا عَنْ رَسُولِ اللَّهِ صَلَّى اللَّهُ عَلَيْهِ
وَسَلَّمَ فِيمَا يَرْوِيهِ عَنْ رَبِّهِ تَبَارَكَ وَتَعَالَى، قَالَ: إِنَّ اللَّهَ كَتَبَ
الْحَسَنَاتِ وَالسَّيِّئَاتِ، ثُمَّ بَيَّنَ ذَلِكَ، فَمَنْ هَمَّ بِحَسَنَةٍ فَلَمْ
يَعْمَلْهَا كَتَبَهَا اللَّهُ عِنْدَهُ حَسَنَةً كَامِلَةً، وَإِنْ هَمَّ بِهَا فَعَمِلَهَا كَتَبَهَا
اللَّهُ عِنْدَهُ عَشْرَ حَسَنَاتٍ إِلَى سَبْعِمائَةِ ضِعْفٍ إِلَى أَضْعَافٍ
كَثِيرَةٍ، وَإِنْ هَمَّ بِسَيِّئَةٍ فَلَمْ يَعْمَلْهَا كَتَبَهَا اللَّهُ عِنْدَهُ حَسَنَةً كَامِلَةً،
وَإِنْ هَمَّ بِهَا فَعَمِلَهَا كَتَبَهَا اللَّهُ سَيِّئَةً وَاحِدَةً.

رَوَاهُ الْبُخَارِيُّ [رقم: ٦٤٩١] وَمُسْلِمٌ [رقم: ١٣١]

On the authority of Ibn ʿAbbās, may God be well pleased
with father and son, who reported that the Messenger of God,
God's blessings and peace be upon him, relating from his Lord said:
'God Most High has decreed good deeds and bad deeds, then He
explained that whoever is on the verge of doing a good deed but
does not do it, God will inscribe it for him as one complete good

deed. And if he goes ahead and does it, He will inscribe it for him as ten good deeds up to seven hundred times or many more times. And if he is on the verge of committing a bad deed but does not do it, God will inscribe it for him as one complete good deed. But if he goes ahead and commits it, God will inscribe it as one bad deed.'

[Narrated by Bukhārī and Muslim]

Look, O my brother, may God give you and me success in His tremendous solicitude, and reflect on these words. The commentators on this prophetic saying have stated that this is a most noble saying in which the Prophet, God's blessings and peace be upon him, explained the extent of God's favour, glory be to Him, to His creation, such that He considers the servant's intention to do a good work to be a good work, even if he does not do it, and He considers his intention to do a bad deed a good deed if he does not go ahead and do it. But if he goes ahead and does it, then God will inscribe it as one single bad deed, while any good deed is inscribed as ten good deeds. It is a tremendous favour that God multiplies good deeds but does not multiply bad ones.

God inscribes the intention of doing a good deed as a good deed because the will to do good is the work of the heart to bind it to that. If it were to be said that this requires that the intention to do a bad deed must be inscribed as a bad deed, for the intention to do something is also of the works of the heart, the answer is that this is not the case, for the person who desists from a bad deed annuls his inclination to sin with another inclination to do good. He has disobeyed his desire to engage in evil and is thereby rewarded for it with a good deed. It is reported in another prophetic saying, 'Indeed he has left it for no other reason except for

My sake.'[73] It is like his saying, God's blessings and peace be upon him, 'charity is incumbent on every single Muslim' They said, 'What if he does not do it?' He said, 'Let him refrain from evil, for that too is a charity.'[74] This prophetic saying is mentioned by Bukhārī in *Kitāb al-Ādāb*. However, abstaining from committing a bad deed is not inscribed as a good deed when one is forced to refrain from committing it or is unable to go ahead with it.

Al-Ṭabarī said, 'There is in this prophetic tradition a confirmation of the thesis of those who say that the guardian angels inscribe the good or bad deeds that the servant in on the verge of doing but does not do, and they know what he thinks. The saying is also a refutation of those who say that the guardian angels inscribe only the outward works of people or that which is heard from them. The meaning of the prophetic saying is therefore that the two angels assigned to every servant know what is going on in his heart. It is possible that God Most High has given them a way to know just as He has enabled His prophets to know many things of the Unseen. God says regarding Jesus, peace be upon him, that he said to the Children of Israel, *I will create for you out of clay as the likeness of a bird; then I will breathe into it, and it will be a bird, by the leave of God. I will also heal the blind and the leper, and bring to life the dead, by the leave of God* [*Āl ʿImrān* 3: 49]. And our Prophet, God's blessings and peace be upon him, has informed of many things of the Unseen. It is therefore possible that God has made a way for the two angels to know what is in the hearts of the children of Adam, whether good or bad, on the basis of which they proceed to inscribe it when they make a resolve to do something.' It is also said that they become aware of what the servant is on the verge of doing through a vapour emitted from the heart.

The pious Predecessors have differed amongst themselves regarding which of the two is better: the remembrance of the heart (or silent remembrance) or loud remembrance. All the above is stated by Ibn Khalaf, better known as Ibn Baṭṭāl. The author of *al-Ifṣāḥ*[75] stated that as God Most High has decreased the length of the life of this community, He compensated it by multiplying its works. So whoever was about to do a good deed will have it counted as one complete good deed, because of his resolve to do something good. God accepts it as a complete good deed so that no one thinks that the mere resolve to do good diminishes his good works and its performance. God has moved it from being a mere resolve into the register of works and inscribed it for the slave as a good deed due to a mere resolve, and then this is multiplied, i.e. this only takes place due to the extent of the intention's sincerity and putting it in its right place.

Then he said after that (*and up to many more times*), i.e., as many times as possible. Here is an example to illustrate the full implication of this noble promise: if a person were to give a grain of wheat in charity, this grain will be counted as far as God's favour is concerned as if it were planted in the best arable land, which is well tended and watered as it deserves to be, upon which, when the time comes, the wheat is harvested. The [grain from this] harvest is then planted the following year in the best arable lands available, which are well tended and watered until they are harvested. The [grain from this] harvest is then planted in the best arable lands, and so on and so forth, until the third year and the fourth year and the year after, continuously until the Day of Judgement. The grain of wheat, mustard or poppy that the servant gives in charity will turn into mighty mountains. Now if any charity is equal to an atom of faith, then one has to consider the profit of what one buys at the time. One can estimate it in the following way: if what is bought is sold in the most sellable market in the biggest country where this thing is widely bought, and then the profit is multiplied until the Day of Judgement, the atom will turn into something as huge as the whole world. All good works in one's dealing with God, exalted is He, are like this when they are the result of sincere intention.

Likewise, God's favour is also multiplied through transfer such as when a person gives a silver coin to a poor man and this man prefers another poor person over himself with this coin, due to his extreme poverty, and the latter does the same with someone who is poorer than him, and so on and so forth, four, five, six times and more. In such a case, God will inscribe for the first person ten silver coins for each coin he gave. When the second person gives those ten silver coins to a third person, what the first one had will go to the second person, i.e. the second person will have ten silver coins, while the first will have a hundred. If the third person gives what he received to a fourth person, he will have ten silver coins in recompense, the second person will have a hundred while the first person who initiated the charity will have a thousand. If the fourth person gives his silver coin in charity, the third person will have a hundred, the second a thousand, while the first person will have ten thousand, and so on and so forth. The first act can be multiplied into a sum only God knows.

Included also in this is when God, glorified and exalted is He, takes His servant to task on the Day of Judgement. If this servant's good deeds are disparate in quality, such that some of them are highly valued while others are less so, God, exalted is He, through His generosity and favour will count all his good deeds as though they were all highly valued. This is because God's generosity surpasses the disparate nature of the good deeds of someone He is well pleased with. God, glorified is He, said in the Qur'ān, *and surely We shall recompense those who were patient their wage, according to the best of what they did* [*al-Naḥl* 16: 97], just as, 'When a servant says in one of the market places of the Muslims, "there is no deity except God, alone without any partner...", raising his voice while doing so, God will inscribe two million good deeds due to this, erase two million of his bad deeds and build a house for him in Paradise.'[76] What we have mentioned is only insofar as the extent of our knowledge goes, not to the extent of God's favour, for He is too great to be denied or circumscribed by anyone.

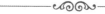

XXXVIII

God's Worship Is a Means to His Nearness and Love

عَنْ أَبِي هُرَيْرَةَ رَضِيَ اللهُ عَنْهُ قَالَ: قَالَ رَسُولُ اللهِ صَلَّى اللهُ عَلَيْهِ وَسَلَّمْ إِنَّ اللهَ تَعَالَىٰ قَالَ: مَنْ عَادَىٰ لِي وَلِيًّا فَقَدْآذَنْتُهُ بِالْحَرْبِ، وَمَا تَقَرَّبَ إِلَيَّ عَبْدِي بِشَيْءٍ أَحَبَّ إِلَيَّ مِمَّا افْتَرَضْتُهُ عَلَيْهِ، وَلَا يَزَالُ عَبْدِي يَتَقَرَّبُ إِلَيَّ بِالنَّوَافِلِ حَتَّىٰ أُحِبَّهُ، فَإِذَا أَحْبَبْتُهُ كُنْتُ سَمْعَهُ الَّذِي يَسْمَعُ بِهِ، وَبَصَرَهُ الَّذِي يُبْصِرُ بِهِ، وَيَدَهُ الَّتِي يَبْطِشُ بِهَا، وَرِجْلَهُ الَّتِي يَمْشِي بِهَا، وَلَئِنْ سَأَلَنِي لَأُعْطِيَنَّهُ، وَلَئِنِ اسْتَعَاذَنِي لَأُعِيذَنَّهُ.

رَوَاهُ الْبُخَارِيُّ [رقم:٦٥٠٢]

On the authority of Abū Hurayrah, may God be well pleased with him, who reported that the Messenger of God, God's blessings and peace be upon him, said, 'Verily God Most High has said: "Whoever shows enmity to a friend of Mine I shall declare war on him. And my servant draws nearer to Me with nothing more beloved to Me than that which I have made obligatory on him. And My servant keeps drawing nearer to Me with supererogatory works until I love him, and when I love him I become his hearing with which he hears, his sight with which he sees, his hands with which he seizes and his legs with which he walks. And if he were to ask Me [for something] I would certainly give it to him, and if he were to seek refuge in Me, I would certainly grant him refuge."'

[Narrated by Bukhārī]

The author of *al-Ifṣāḥ* wrote, 'One can understand from this Prophetic saying that God warns all those who show enmity towards the friends of God that He will declare war on them because of this display of enmity. The friend of God Most High is him who follows His Sacred Law. Let one therefore beware of hurting the hearts of God's friends.'

However, I do not think the meaning of this saying refers to other than showing enmity towards a friend of God merely because of his friendship with God. As for when circumstances require a dispute between two friends of God, or a contention regarding extracting a right that is not apparent, such matters are not included in the meaning of this prophetic saying. Abū Bakr al-Ṣiddīq and ʿUmar ibn al-Khaṭṭāb, for example, had a dispute,[77] so did al-ʿAbbās and ʿAlī ibn Abī Ṭālib,[78] as did many other prophetic Companions, may God be well pleased with all of them.

His saying (*And My servant draws nearer to Me with nothing more beloved to Me than that which I have made obligatory on him*) contains an allusion to the fact that a supererogatory act should not take precedence over an obligatory one. Supererogatory acts of worship are called so because they are something that one does in surplus, after completing that which is obligatory; otherwise, they would not be called supererogatory. This is evidenced by His saying (*And My servant keeps drawing nearer to Me with supererogatory works until I love him*) because drawing nearer to God with supererogatory works happens only after completing what is obligated. When a servant persists in drawing nearer to God through supererogatory works, this will lead to his being loved by God, exalted is He.

He said (*And when I love him I become his hearing with which he hears, his sight with which he sees...*). This is the sign of God's friendship for the one who had not been loved by Him. What this means is that he will not listen to anything the Sacred Law has not permitted, he will not look at anything the Sacred Law has disallowed, he will not extend his hands towards something the Sacred Law has made unlawful, and he will not go to any place that the Sacred Law has not sanctioned. In principle, this is what the question is all about. However, a servant may be so overwhelmed by God's remembrance that he becomes known by this feature, such that when he is addressed with other than God's remembrance he can hardly hear those addressing him until the latter, who are not among the folk of God, approach him with the remembrance of God as a means for him to listen to them. The same applies to that which is seen, seized with the hands or walked to. This is a very lofty trait, and we ask God Most High to make us among those who possess it.

His saying (*And if he were to seek refuge in Me, I would certainly grant him refuge*) indicates that when a servant becomes among the folk whom God loves, this does not stop him from asking God for all his needs or seeking refuge in Him from those he might fear. God Most High is capable of giving him before asking and granting him refuge before him requesting Him. However, God, glorified is He, draws close to his servants by fulfilling the requests of those who ask Him and granting refuge to those who seek it from Him.

XXXIX

Excusing the Person who Errs, Forgets or Is Coerced

عَنْ ابْنِ عَبَّاسٍ رَضِيَ اللَّهُ عَنْهُمَا أَنَّ رَسُولَ اللَّهِ صَلَّى اللَّهُ عَلَيْهِ وَسَلَّمْ قَالَ: إِنَّ اللَّهَ تَجَاوَزَ لِي عَنْ أُمَّتِي الْخَطَأَ وَالنِّسْيَانَ وَمَا اسْتُكْرِهُوا عَلَيْهِ.

رَوَاهُ ابْنُ مَاجَهْ [رقم:٢٠٤٥] وَالْبَيْهَقِيِّ [رقم: ٧]

On the authority of Ibn ʿAbbās, may God be well pleased with father and son, who reported that the Messenger of God, God's blessings and peace be upon him, said: 'For my sake, God has excused my nation in relation to erring, forgetting and that which they have been coerced to do.'

[Narrated by Ibn Mājah and Bayhaqī]

It is mentioned in the commentary of God's words, *Whether you publish what is in your hearts or hide it, God shall make reckoning with you for it* [al-Baqarah 2: 284], that when this verse was revealed, the prophetic Companions, may God be well pleased with all of them, felt that it was too hard on them. A group of them, including Abū Bakr, ʿUmar, ʿAbd al-Raḥman ibn ʿAwf and Muʿādh ibn Jabal, went to the Messenger of God, God's blessings and peace be upon him, and said, 'Works have been enjoined upon us that are more we can bear. We do indeed talk inwardly to ourselves with things we dislike to remain in our hearts and we also have the matter of this world.' So the Prophet, God's blessings and peace be upon him, said: 'Perhaps you are saying as the Children of Israel have said, "We hear and disobey"; rather say, "We hear and obey."' This was too hard for the prophetic Companions who remained in this situation for a whole year. Then God Most High sent His relief and mercy with His words, *God charges no soul save to its capacity; standing to its account is what it has earned, and against its account what it has merited* [*al-Baqarah* 2: 286], to which He said: 'I have done so!' And so ease on the Muslim community descended and the first Qurānic verse was abrogated.

Al-Bayhaqī quoted Imām Shāfiʿī as saying, 'God, glorified and exalted is He, says, *excepting him who has been compelled, and his heart is still at rest in his belief* [*al-Naḥl* 16: 106], and disbelief has legal prescriptions related to it. So when God has excused such a person, the prescriptions of coercion were forfeited regarding all statements. This is because when what is great is forfeited, what is less is also forfeited.' Then Imām Shāfiʿī related from Ibn ʿAbbās through his own chain of transmission that God's Messenger, God's blessings and peace be upon him, said, 'For my sake, God has excused my nation in relation to erring, forgetting and that which they have been coerced to do.'

He also related through his own chain of transmission on the authority of ʿĀ'ishah, may God be well pleased with her, that the Messenger of God, God's blessings and peace be upon him, said, 'Divorce and slave manumission do not take place under coercion.'[79] This is the adopted opinion of ʿUmar ibn al-Khaṭṭāb, Ibn ʿUmar and Ibn al-Zubayr. It is reported that Thābit ibn al-Aḥnaf married the emancipated slave of ʿAbd al-Raḥmān ibn Zayd ibn al-Khaṭṭāb after bearing a child from the latter. ʿAbd al-Raḥmān ibn Zayd forced Thābit ibn al-Aḥnaf with the whip and threats to divorce his wife. This took place during the caliphate of Ibn al-Zubayr. However, Ibn ʿUmar told Thābit ibn al-Aḥnaf that the divorce was void and that he could go back to his wife. Ibn al-Zubayr was at that time in Makkah and Thābit joined him there to inform him of the situation. Ibn al-Zubayr wrote to his governor in Madīnah to return Thābit's wife to him and to punish ʿAbd al-Raḥmān ibn Zayd. So Ṣafiyyah bint Abī ʿUbayd, the wife of ʿAbd Allāh ibn ʿUmar, helped Thābit's wife to get ready for her husband, and ʿAbd Allāh ibn ʿUmar attended his wedding party. And God knows best.

This World Is a
Means and a Plantation
for the Afterlife

عَنْ ابْنِ عُمَرَ رَضِيَ اللَّهُ عَنْهُمَا قَالَ: أَخَذَ رَسُولُ اللَّهِ صَلَّى اللَّهُ
عَلَيْهِ وَسَلَّمْ بِمَنْكِبَيَّ، وَقَالَ: كُنْ فِي الدُّنْيَا كَأَنَّكَ غَرِيبٌ
أَوْ عَابِرُ سَبِيلٍ. وَكَانَ ابْنُ عُمَرَ رَضِيَ اللَّهُ عَنْهُمَا يَقُولُ: إِذَا
أَمْسَيْتَ فَلَا تَنْتَظِرِ الصَّبَاحَ، وَإِذَا أَصْبَحْتَ فَلَا تَنْتَظِرِ الْمَسَاءَ،
وَخُذْ مِنْ صِحَّتِكَ لِمَرَضِكَ، وَمِنْ حَيَاتِكَ لِمَوْتِكَ.

رَوَاهُ الْبُخَارِيُّ [رقم:٦٤١٦]

On the authority of Ibn 'Umar, may God be well pleased with
father and son, who reported that the Messenger of God, God's
blessings and peace be upon him, took him by his shoulders
and said: 'Be in this world as a stranger or a traveller passing
through.' The son of 'Umar, may God be well pleased with father
and son, used to say, 'When you reach the evening, do not anticipate the arrival of the morning; and when you reach the morning,

do not anticipate the arrival of the evening. And take from your health for your sickness and from your life for your death.'

[Narrated by Bukhārī]

Imām Abū'l-Ḥasan ʿAlī ibn Khalaf in his commentary on Bukhārī quoted Abū'l-Zinād as saying, 'This prophetic saying means that one is encouraged to mix less with others, have less possessions and be unattached to this world.' Abū'l-Ḥasan continued, 'As an explanation to this one may say that the stranger is less open to people and is further alienated from them, for he hardly passes by anyone he knows or able to mix with someone whom he can find fellowship with. Rather, he is always abased, and fearful. And the same applies to the traveller passing through who manages his journey as he has the ability to do so due to the lightness of the things he carries with him and his lack of concern for anything that may hinder him from completing his journey. The believer too does not need anything from this world except that which helps him reach his final destination.'

Abū Hurayrah, may God be well pleased with him, said, 'There is in this prophetic saying that which indicates that the Messenger of God, God's blessings and peace be upon him, encourages the emulation of the stranger, for when the latter enters a town he neither competes with its inhabitants in their assemblies, nor does he mind being seen wearing what he does not customarily wear, nor does he turn his back on the people of this town because of enmity or grudges. Likewise, the traveller passing through neither acquires a home, nor does he engage in disputes with people, nor start feuds with them: he knows that he will only stay with them for a few days and then move on. All the states of the stranger and the traveller passing through are recommended for the believer in this world. This is because this world is not an abode of residence for him: it only prevents him from his real abode and comes further between him and his final dwelling place.

As for the saying of Ibn ʿUmar, (*When you reach the evening, do not anticipate the morning, and when you reach the morning, do not anticipate reaching the evening*), it is his encouragement to the believer to always prepare for death. Preparation for death is through righteous works. Ibn ʿUmar also encourages the believer not to have high hopes, i.e., one should not defer the works of the night until the morning but rather hasten to do them in their due time. And likewise, when one reaches the morning, one should not delay the works due at that time until the evening or the night.

His saying (*And take from your health for your sickness*) is an encouragement to take advantage of one's health to strive in achieving good works for fear of the advent of sickness that will prevent one from work. Likewise his saying (*And take from your life for your death*) is a warning to seize the opportunity of the days of one's life, for one's work will cease when one dies, one's hopes will be dashed and one's regrets for one's slackness will also be great. One should know that a long time will come when one is under the soil, unable to perform any works, and incapable of remembering God, glorified is He. So, one must hasten during the time of one's well-being to do righteous works. How comprehensive is this prophetic saying as it combines all the loftiest meanings of goodness!

A scholar said, 'God Most High has censured hope and its prolongation, saying, *leave them to eat, and to take their joy, and to be bemused by hope; certainly they will soon know!* [*al-Ḥijr* 15: 3]. ʿAlī ibn Abī Ṭālib, may God be well pleased with him, said, 'This world has departed and is going backward and the Afterlife has departed and is coming forward and each has children. So be among the children of the Afterlife and do not be among the children of this world. For today there is work and no reckoning and tomorrow there will be reckoning and no work.'[80]

Anas, may God be well pleased with him, said, 'The Prophet, God's blessings and peace be upon him, drew lines [on the sand] and then said: 'This is man, this is his hope and this is his moment of death. As he is in the process of hoping the closest line gets to him',[81] which is the moment of his death surrounding him. This is a warning to shorten one's hopes and anticipate one's moment of death for fear of its suddenness. And as one's moment of death is unknown to one, it is befitting that one expects it and waits for it, lest it overtake one while in a state of heedlessness and unguardedness. Therefore, let the believer train himself to pay heed to what he is warned about and to resist his hopes and wanton desires, for it is the innate nature of humans to harbour hope. ᶜAbd Allāh ibn ᶜUmar may God be well pleased with him and his father [ᶜUmar ibn al-Khaṭṭāb], said, 'The Messenger of God, God's blessings and peace be upon him, saw me covering the walls of a walled garden that belonged to me and my mother, so he said: "What is this, O ᶜAbd Allāh?" I said, "O Messenger of God, the wall is falling down, so we are repairing it!" He said: "I can see only that the matter [the instant of leaving this world] is much closer than that."'[82]

We ask God the Mighty to be solicitous with us and to make us unattached to this world and to make us desire only that which is with Him and to find our repose on the Day of Judgement, He is indeed Magnanimous, Generous, Forgiving and Most Compassionate.

XLI

The Sign of Faith

عَنْ أَبِي مُحَمَّدٍ عَبْدِ اللهِ بْنِ عَمْرِو بْنِ الْعَاصِ رَضِيَ اللهُ عَنْهُمَا،
قَالَ: قَالَ رَسُولُ اللهِ صَلَّى اللهُ عَلَيْهِ وَسَلَّمْ: لَا يُؤْمِنُ أَحَدُكُمْ
حَتَّىٰ يَكُونَ هَوَاهُ تَبَعًا لِمَا جِئْتُ بِهِ.

رَوَاهُ الْحَكِيمُ التِّرْمِذِيُّ فِي نَوَادِرِ الأُصُول

On the authority of Abū Muhammad ʿAbd Allāh ibn ʿAmr ibn al-ʿĀṣ, may God be well pleased with father and son, who reported that the Messenger of God, God's blessings and peace be upon him, said: 'None of you shall truly believe until his desire conforms to that which I have brought.'

[Narrated by al-Ḥakīm al-Tirmidhī in *Nawādir al-Uṣūl*]

This prophetic saying is like the words of God, glorified and exalted is He, *But no, by thy Lord! They will not believe till they make thee the judge regarding the disagreement between them* [*al-Nisā'* 4: 65]. The occasion of this verse's revelation is the following: al-Zubayr, may God be well pleased with him, had a dispute with a man from the Madīnan Helpers regarding the distribution of water, and they took their dispute to the Messenger of God, God's blessings and peace be upon him. The Prophet, God's blessings and peace be upon him, said: 'O Zubayr! Water [your land] and then release the water for your neighbour', thus prompting him to be forgiving and easy-going with his neighbour. But then the Madīnan Helper retorted, 'You are saying this only because he is your maternal cousin!' On hearing this, the face of the Messenger of God, God's blessings and peace be upon him, changed in anger and he said: 'O Zubayr, retain the water until it reaches the root, then you can release it.'[83] This is because the first judgement of the Messenger of God, God's peace and blessings be upon him, was delivered with consideration for the benefit of the Madīnan Helper. However, when the Madīnan Helper angered him, he directed al-Zubayr to take full advantage of his right, and so this verse was revealed.

It is also rigorously reported from the Prophet, God's blessings and peace be upon him, in another saying that he said: 'By Him in whose Hand is my soul, none of you shall truly believe until I become more beloved to him than his father, children and all the people.'[84] Abū'l-Zinād said, 'This is of the comprehensive speech for he has combined in these few words numerous meanings. This is because love is divided into three subdivisions: love due to respect and esteem, like love for one's father; love due to compassion and pity, like love for one's children; and love due to appreciation and likeness, like love for all people. And so the few words of the prophetic saying have circumscribed all these different kinds of love.'

Ibn Baṭṭāl wrote, 'This saying means, and God knows best, that whoever has perfected his faith knows that the right and merit of the Messenger of God, God's blessings and peace be upon him, are more stressed upon him than the rights of his father, children and all other people. For it is through the Messenger, God's blessings and peace be upon him, that God has saved him from the Fire and guided him after he was lost in misguidance.' What is meant by this prophetic saying is spending one's self for him, God's blessings and peace be upon him. The prophetic Companions, may God be pleased with them, used to fight at his side against their fathers, children and brothers. Abū ʿUbaydah killed his father for harming the Messenger of God, God's blessings and peace be upon him. Abū Bakr al-Ṣiddīq, may God be well pleased with him, also sought out his father at the Battle of Badr in an attempt to kill him. Whoever finds this quality within himself, his desires truly conform to that which is brought by the Prophet, God's blessings and peace be upon him.

XLII

The Vastness of God's Mercy

عَنْ أَنَسٍ رَضِيَ اللَّهُ عَنْهُ قَالَ: سَمِعْتُ رَسُولَ اللَّهِ صَلَّى اللَّهُ عَلَيْهِ وَسَلَّمَ يَقُولُ: قَالَ اللَّهُ تَعَالَى: يَا ابْنَ آدَمَ! إِنَّكَ مَا دَعَوْتَنِي وَرَجَوْتَنِي غَفَرْتُ لَكَ عَلَى مَا كَانَ مِنْكَ وَلَا أُبَالِي. يَا ابْنَ آدَمَ! لَوْ بَلَغَتْ ذُنُوبُكَ عَنَانَ السَّمَاءِ ثُمَّ اسْتَغْفَرْتَنِي غَفَرْتُ لَكَ. يَا ابْنَ آدَمَ! إِنَّكَ لَوْ أَتَيْتَنِي بِقُرَابِ الْأَرْضِ خَطَايَا ثُمَّ لَقِيتَنِي لَا تُشْرِكُ بِي شَيْئًا لَأَتَيْتُكَ بِقُرَابِهَا مَغْفِرَةً.

رَوَاهُ التِّرْمِذِيُّ [رقم: ٣٥٤٠]

On the authority of Anas, may God be well pleased with him, who reported that he heard the Messenger of God, God's blessings and peace be upon him say: 'God Most High says, "O son of Adam! Verily, as long as you beseech Me and have hope in Me, I shall forgive you no matter what has ensued from you and I shall not mind. O son of Adam! If your sins were to reach the clouds in the sky and you were to ask forgiveness from Me, I shall forgive you. O son of Adam! If you were to come to me with sins the size of the earth and then encountered Me, while not associating anything with Me, I shall come to you with forgiveness the size of the earth."'

[Narrated by Tirmidhī]

There is in this prophetic saying a tremendous glad tiding, great clemency and generosity as well as innumerable types of favour, beneficence, tenderness, mercy and bestowal of bounties. Similar to this is the saying of the Prophet, God's blessings and peace be upon him: 'Verily, God is more happy with the repentance of His servant than one of you with his long-searched-for object were he to find it.'[85]

It is related that Abū Ayyūb, may God be well pleased with him, said when he was on the verge of death, 'I have kept something from you that I heard from God's Messenger, God's peace and blessings be upon him, [that I will relate to you now]. He said: "If it had not been the case that you sin, God would have created beings who sin and whom He would then forgive."'[86] There are many other prophetic sayings that agree with this tradition.

His saying (*O son of Adam! As long as you beseech Me and have hope in Me*) is in conformity with His words, 'I am as My servant thinks of Me, so let him think of Me what he wills.'[87] It is also related in another tradition that, 'When the servant commits a sin and has remorse about it, saying, "O my Lord! I have committed a sin, so please forgive me, for none forgives sins except You." God Most High will respond, "My servant knew that he has a Lord who forgives sins and punishes due to them. I take you as a witness that I have forgiven him." The servant than com-mits a sin and says the same thing twice and thrice, and God Most High will say the same on each and every occasion, after which He will say: "Do as you will, I have forgiven you"', i.e., because you have committed a sin and sought My forgiveness for it.

Know also that repentance has three conditions: desisting from contravention, regretting the contravention that one has committed and resolving not to return to it. If the contravention relates to the right of another human being, then one must hasten to return his right and request his forgiveness. If the contravention is between one and God Most High and involves an act of expiation, then one must make the expiation, in which case this is a fourth condition. If a person were to do the like of this repeatedly during the day and repent by fulfilling all the conditions of repentance, then God will forgive him.

His saying (*O son of Adam! If your sins were to reach the clouds in the sky and you were then to ask My forgiveness, I shall forgive you*) means if your sins were like individuals filling the space between the heaven and earth – which is a vast multitude – His generosity, clemency and forgiveness would still be far greater than that. In fact, there is neither correspondence of any kind between God's generosity and forgiveness and the extent of people's sins, nor does preference between the two enter into question here at all: the sins of mankind simply wane into nothingness when compared with His clemency and pardon.

Regarding his saying (*O son of Adam! If you were to come to me with sins the like of the earth and encountered Me, while not associating anything with Me, I shall come to you with forgiveness the like of the earth*), 'encountered Me' means to die upon faith, not associating anything or anyone with Him. Indeed, there is no repose for the believer without the encounter with his Lord. God Most High says, *God forgives not that aught should be with Him associated; less than that He forgives to whomsoever He will* [*al-Nisā'* 4: 48]. The Prophet, God's blessings and peace be upon him, said: 'He is not persistent [in sinning] who asks for forgiveness even if he sins again and again, seventy times a day',[88] and Abū Hurayrah, may God be well pleased with him, reported that the Messenger of God, God's blessings and peace be upon him, said: 'Having a good opinion of God is the result of worshipping Him well'.[89]

Endnotes

1 Narrated by Ṭabarānī in *al-Awsaṭ* from Abū Hurayrah.

2 Narrated by Bukhārī and Muslim.

3 Narrated by Bukhārī and Muslim.

4 Narrated by Bukhārī and Muslim.

5 Narrated by Abū Dāwūd.

6 Narrated by Tirmidhī.

7 Narrated by Bukhārī.

8 Narrated by Bukhārī.

9 Narrated by Bukhārī.

10 Narrated by Bukhārī.

11 Narrated by Muslim.

12 Narrated by al-Nasā'ī.

13 Narrated by Bukhārī and Muslim.

14 Narrated by Bukhārī.

15 Narrated by Nasā'ī.

16 Narrated by Bukhārī.

17 Narrated by Muslim.

18 Narrated by Tirmidhī.

19 Narrated by Ibn Ḥibbān.

20 Narrated by Ibn Abī Ḥātim.

21 Narrated by Muslim.

22 In their commentaries on this *ḥadīth*, several classical authorities, including Ibn Rajab al-Ḥanbalī, stress the general principle laid down here – the protection of life in a Muslim society in the context of Muslim governance – rather than the three exceptions, as Ibn Daqīq al-ʿĪd does in his commentary. – Editors.

23 Historically, this was an official state process, and was not interpreted as a licence for vigilantism; and Muslims are, in any case, duty bound to abide by the law of the land in which they live. Some

scholars distinguish between apostasy and treason against the state, the former being a capital punishment in the early Muslim state but was understood later on as a matter between the individual and God, and not as a matter of criminal law. For instance, the early Shāfiʿīs, including Imām al-Shāfiʿī, and the Ḥanafīs did *not* consider the punishment for the apostate (*murtadd*) applicable to one who had privately left Islam. In this context, these scholars distinguished between the broad Qurānic worldview that upholds freedom of religion, which is underpinned by its ethical teachings on individual accountability and responsibility, and apostasy as a political act that aimed at harming the integrity of the Muslim polity. – Editors.

24 Narrated by Bukhārī and Muslim.

25 See footnote 23 above for clarification about the issue of applying penal law in Islam. Classical commentators such as Ibn Rajab al-Ḥanbalī emphasize that this prophetic report underlines the importance of the protection of individual, public and family life from potential harms (in the context of a Muslim society). Adultery has such harmful consequences, as it essentially threatens the integrity of progeny and the safety of family life, and needs to be prevented. Although, the Qur'ān does *not* prescribe stoning (*rajm*), classical Muslim scholars argued that it was once part of the Qur'ān but was later abrogated. They contended that prophetic reports contain evidence to suggest that *rajm* was practised, albeit on a few occasions during the Prophet's lifetime. He was reluctant to punish even those who confessed to adultery. He allowed them to repent and think through their confession. Under Islamic law, the level of evidence required for enact *rajm* is so demanding that the actual enactments of *rajm* were minute in Muslim history. Instead, the legal and religious authorities often exercised discretion to ward off the application of *rajm* due to problems with the evidence. In practice, therefore, the threat of *rajm* was meant to be exemplary and preventive rather than routinized as punishment. In any case, this whole discussion assumes the presence of an Islamic political and legal authority that is not applicable today. – Editors.

26 Narrated by Bukhārī.

27 See footnote 23 above for clarification about the issue of applying penal law in Islam. Classical commentators such as Ibn Rajab al-Hanbali discussed the presence of dissenting voices in this debate such as the Hanafis, the most widespread legal school in Sunni Islam, who viewed non-Muslims as equal in law (in cases of retribution or *qiṣāṣ*). In terms of gender, there is clear agreement that Muslim men and women have equal rights in terms of *qiṣāṣ*. The principle of expiation (*kaffārah*) in classical Islamic law was always used to free slaves but this impetus towards freedom was only brought to fruition in the nineteenth century when slavery was largely abolished in Muslim-majority lands. Of course, underlying the case for the equality of all human life is the principal statement in the Qur'ān that the killing of one soul (*nafs*) is equivalent of killing alll of humankind (*al-Mā'idah* 5: 32). – Editors.

28 Narrated by Aḥmad and Tirmidhī.

29 Narrated by Tirmidhī.

30 Narrated by Bukhārī.

31 Narrated by Bukhārī.

32 Narrated by Tirmidhī.

33 Narrated by Aḥmad.

34 Narrated by Bukhārī.

35 If even in the very worst of acts, such as killing, the Muslim is reminded to preserve the principle of kindness, then kindness should inform her or his acts in every imaginable circumstance in life. This *ḥadīth* was one of the key source-texts used by the classical scholars to define in legal terms what the exercise of restraint in war entailed, such as not harming non-combatants, women, children and prisoners of war. – Editors.

36 Narrated by Tirmidhī.

37 Narrated by Ṭabarānī.

38 Narrated by Aḥmad.

39 Narrated by Bukhārī.

40 Narrated by Tirmidhī.

41 Narrated by Muslim.

42 Mentioned by Ibn Kathīr in his commentary of *Sūrah al-Anbiyā'*.

43 Narrated by Abū Dāwūd.

44 Narrated by Tirmidhī.

45 Narrated by Tirmidhī.

46 Narrated by Aḥmad. Its continuation is, 'and know that your best work is the prayer and none remains in a state of *wuḍū'* except a believer.'

47 Narrated by Muslim.

48 Narrated by Bukhārī.

49 Narrated by Bukhārī.

50 The Ẓāhirites (al-Ẓāhiriyyah) were a small trend within Islamic legal thought that rejected analogy, believing that only the apparent or manifest meanings of the Qur'ān and *aḥādīth* were valid. The movement largely died out in the medieval period.

51 Narrated by Tirmidhī.

52 Narrated by Tirmidhī.

53 Narrated by Ibn Mājah.

54 Narrated by Bukhārī.

55 Narrated by Tirmidhī.

56 Narrated by Bukhārī.

57 Narrated by Bukhārī.

58 Narrated by Muslim.

59 Narrated by Tirmidhī.

60 Narrated by Bayhaqī.

61 Narrated by Ṭabarānī.

62 A saying attributed to ʿAlī ibn Abī Ṭālib.

63 Narrated by Tirmidhī.

64 Narrated by Muslim.

65 Narrated by Bukhārī.

66 Narrated by Tirmidhī.

67 Narrated by Muslim.

68 Narrated by Muslim.

69 Narrated by Muslim.

70 Narrated by Abū Dāwūd.

71 Narrated by Bukhārī.

72 Narrated by Abū Dāwūd.

73 Narrated by Muslim.

74 Narrated by Bukhārī.

75 The vizier and scholar ʿAwn al-Dīn Abū'l-Muẓaffar Yaḥyā ibn Muhammad ibn Hubayrah the Ḥanbalite (d. 560 AH).

76 Narrated by Tirmidhī.

77 Narrated by Bukhārī.

78 Narrated by Bukhārī.

79 Narrated by Abū Dāwūd.

80 Narrated by Bukhārī.

81 Narrated by Bukhārī.

82 Narrated by Tirmidhī.

83 Narrated by Bukhārī.

84 Narrated by Bukhārī.

85 Narrated by Muslim.

86 Narrated by Muslim.

87 Narrated by Bukhārī.

88 Narrated by Abū Dāwūd.

89 Narrated by Abū Dāwūd.

Index

H

I

J

K

L

M

N

O

P

Q

Z